the daily soup cookbook

the daily soup cook book

Leslie Kaul, Bob Spiegel,
Carla Ruben, and Peter Siegel with Robin Vitetta-Miller

FALL RIVER PRESS

Fall River Press
122 Fifth Avenue
New York, NY 10011

ISBN-13: 978-1-4351-0942-1
ISBN-10: 1-4351-0942-2

Printed and bound in the United States of America

1 3 5 7 9 10 8 6 4 2

TO MY MOTHER,
MY MUSIC TEACHER,
MY AUNT . . .
REGINA SPIEGEL

CONTENTS

INTRODUCTION

WE ALL HAVE a special "someone" who makes the *best* soup. Whether it's your mother's, your grandmother's or your best friend's, there's just something about *that* soup that tastes better than anyone else's. And the aroma and flavor of that soup arouses all kinds of emotions and thoughts that remind us of happier days. For some people, a hot bowl of tomato soup conjures up images of snowy mornings (and subsequent school closings). For others, clam chowder means a summer vacation and cool nights on the beach. And, of course, we all have at least one relative who relies on chicken soup as a cure-all. Soup soothes, comforts, and nourishes. Soup is important.

It's not just modern lore; soup dates back to the caveman—even Fred Flintstone ate soup. And lentil soup, the forefather of all soups, was discovered as early as 8,000 B.C.—followed quickly by the invention of the spoon.

Regardless of nationality or culture, everyone has an attachment to soup, and everyone has a favorite. But, your beloved cream of mushroom soup may be unrecognizable to the cream of mushroom aficionado up the block. And the tomato rice buff who lives next door may think you're both crazy. We're not saying the split pea people can't get along with the navy bean people, it's just that everyone has a strong opinion about soup.

Regardless of what ails us, from a hectic work schedule to feeling "under the weather," a bowl of soup makes us feel better. You rarely hear anyone emphatically say, "I don't like soup," and the person who does cannot be trusted.

At Daily Soup, soup is our life. All we serve is soup. All we talk about is soup. We even dream about soup. Every day we create, renovate, improve, and adjust our soups. We plan each day's menu based on a balance of color, texture, body, and seasoning so that we have something for everyone. We listen to our customers (all soup connoisseurs by now) and they give us constant feedback. We learn from their traditions and ancestry and integrate their knowledge into our recipes.

Our recipes are inspired by grandmothers from all over the world—we're just soup brokers. We keep tradition alive by enhancing cherished recipes with our five-star restaurant expertise, and we pass these creations on to our customers. These soups represent dozens of cultures, originating in trattorias, bistros, and chili parlors, Indian roadside stands, Cajun backwoods picnics, Thai fisherman's dinners, and New England wharf-side chowderfests. To understand the range of our recipes, imagine what a menu board would look like if every dignitary at the United Nations brought in his or her grandmother's recipe.

The four basic soup classifications are usually *broth*, *thick*, *clear*, and *pureed*. But, at Daily Soup, we've blurred the lines between categories. Our broth soups are thick and chunky, our thick soups are pureed, and we don't serve anything clear. We organize our soups to give customers what they want—Vegetarian, Seafood, Meat, Low Fat, Dairy Free, and Spicy. We offer potato, corn, tomato, grain, nut, cheese and bean soups (see A Note on Organization, page 8). We take classic soups and give them a twist, such as adding seafood to our Minestrone, sweet Italian sausage to our Split Pea, and chicken to our Wild Mushroom Barley. We experiment all the time, but we try not to combine ingredients from different parts of the world because the flavors often don't blend. Otherwise, we'd have soups like Miso-Matzoh Ball or Borscht with Corn Tortillas.

"Is it a meal?" That's the first question we ask ourselves when we develop our soups. Traditional first-course soups, such as Lobster Bisque and Vichyssoise, required the liberal addition of vegetables and chunks of lobster meat before they qualified as *meals*. Soups or stews that were already main courses, such as Jambalaya, Chicken Pot Pie, and Chili Con Carne, were made extra thick. How thick? Thick enough to hold a spoon upright, and thick enough to make a soup sandwich with a hunk of bread.

All of our soups are batch-cooked, which is the way soups were traditionally made in the peasant culture from which they were derived. They are not cooked in assembly lines or production houses. As is true with many cultures, we share the ultimate pursuit of flavor. We take no shortcuts and we use the finest regional ingredients, including fresh Maine lobster, Alaskan king crab, grade A chicken, and market fresh produce. And, all of our soup stocks are made from scratch.

Our customers come to Daily Soup for various reasons. Many of our regulars come in four to five times per week. They either want something new or something familiar, and we have it all—old favorites, variations of classics, and eclectic newcomers that boast exotic, innovative flavors. We always

3

encourage sampling and everyone is welcome to taste several of our soups. Since our menu changes daily, and fifteen to twenty new recipes are added each month, it would be difficult to make a decision based solely on the look and clever name of the soup. Tasting different soups helps our customers make their selection, while introducing them to new flavor combinations.

We've been asked repeatedly to write a cookbook and each time we've declined. We figured, "We have over five hundred soups—no book of soup recipes should be longer than the Bible." We finally reconsidered. Why? It was time to get some of these recipes off our chests. We couldn't live with the guilt, knowing we were hoarding such valuable treasures. So we gathered together our favorite and most popular concoctions and put them into a manageable collection. We've created a book with a full range of soup recipes, so you can maximize your soup potential.

DAILY SOUP
soup company

SOUP

HOW TO USE THIS BOOK

GOOD COOKING REQUIRES common sense and instinct. Our soup recipes are not like elaborate instructions for building an atomic bomb. If you change ingredients or alter proportions, you won't ignite an explosion. The recipes are foundations designed to encourage creativity. Soup is a compilation of ingredients, and trying to duplicate exact measurements time after time would be mathematically impossible. So, relax—whatever your soup tastes like—it's correct. It's your interpretation. Soup is flexible and forgiving, and you won't ruin any of the recipes. Unless, of course, you don't strain the stock, undercook the beans, forget to cut the vegetables, or go on vacation while your soup is cooking.

KNOW YOUR INGREDIENTS

To make your soup even more forgiving, it's important that you understand the effect each ingredient has on the final outcome. If you use the same ingredients, but change the order of when they're added to the pot, you will get a completely different flavor. For example, garlic can be sautéed at the beginning to create garlic-infused oil that transports flavor throughout the soup from the start; it can be roasted whole and added midway through cooking (for a rich, mellow taste); or minced garlic cloves can be added raw at the end for a pungent, spicy burst.

7

A NOTE ON ORGANIZATION

There is no perfect or "right" way to categorize soup. The minute you start to stereotype a soup, you walk a thin line. Some people have tried to organize soups by country or region of origin, by consistency (brothy or thick), by crustacean, beef, or game, by the complexity of its cooking process, by season or holiday, by diet, and by temperature.

We have categorized our soups based on the primary way we look at them when we are planning an all-soup menu: by the main ingredient. For example, nut-based soups are in the Nut chapter and coconut-infused soups are in the Coconut chapter. We just find it an easy way to lay out the soups. We then note which of them are spicy, lowfat, vegetarian, and so on. Since our soups are composed of so many ingredients, there will always be crossovers between categories—some soups in the Chili chapter have beans, some soups in the Cheese chapter have potatoes. We're not saying our way is "right," but it works.

THE IMPORTANCE OF TASTE

Taste is what gives food its personality, and soup should have a likable personality, not multiple ones. Our soups are flavorful but not complex. The main ingredient in any soup should be recognizable and not muted by other flavors. For example, the cantaloupe in our Thai Melon with Peanuts (page 182) is the headliner, while the herbs, spices, and peanuts are the supporting cast. The additional flavors all have their own distinct personality, but their role is to accentuate the melon, not overpower it.

ALLOW PLENTY OF TIME

Time is an important ingredient because soup changes character with each stage of the cooking process. Flavors change as ingredients react and blend with one another. That's what makes soup so fascinating—it constantly evolves and becomes something new. In baking, nothing changes after the ingredients are mixed and baked. With soup, you can start, stop, change, fix, and enhance the mixture anywhere in the cooking process. The smell and taste will guide you, and there's plenty of room for improvisation and creativity.

ADD LOTS OF LOVE

Finally, love is the most important ingredient of all. Love is preparing food for someone else with the same attention to detail you would give to yourself. That means making sure the chicken stock is intensely flavored, the shrimp are abundant, and the best bowl in the house is not for you. Love is the simple act of combining fine ingredients, watching them blend and change, drooling (not into the soup) from the aroma, and, of course, enjoying the finished product. A soup without love is no soup at all. As the Beatles said at the end of *Abbey Road,* "The love you take is equal to the love you make." A song written, by the way, over a hot bowl of borscht.

SOME THINGS TO REMEMBER

TEMPERATURE

Soups and stocks should come to a full boil (212 degrees) to kill any bacteria.
Then, the heat should be reduced to a simmer (about 185 degrees, or when
bubbles just break the surface). This gentle cooking temperature prevents
scorching and extracts the full flavor from the ingredients without breaking
them apart.

Temperature is very important when cooking and cooling soup. Since soup
changes temperature many times during the cooking process, bacteria has an
opportunity to grow. Strive to keep the temperature above 165 degrees to kill
any bacteria. Each time you add a new ingredient, the overall temperature
reduces and you're essentially reheating the soup. When the soup is finished
cooking, you have a maximum of four hours to bring the temperature down to
38 to 40 degrees (if you don't plan to eat immediately). To cool large containers of soup, immerse the pot in an ice-water bath first to "shock" and cool the
soup before refrigerating.

FREEZING

Almost all soups freeze well. Since soup expands when frozen, fill air-tight
containers three quarters full, rather than completely filling them to the top.
Ice crystals form between 26 and 32 degrees, so to prevent them, you must get

to 26 degrees as fast as possible (ice crystals form not only in the body of the soup, but inside the vegetables and meat as well, so when you reheat the soup, the ingredients all have a mealy texture). To reach 26 degrees quickly, refrigerate soup first (to reach 45 degrees) and then freeze the soup in small batches. Soup is best stored in the freezer no longer than 2 months at 0 to 10 degrees. This may sound obvious, but always reheat frozen soup before eating it. And, once a soup has been defrosted and reheated, it's best not to freeze it again. You can try, but you'll end up reheating a bland soup with a mushy texture. We know, it's hard to part with a good soup.

STOCKS

All of our stocks are located in the back of the book. We use our own stocks in all of our soups, and we encourage you to make your own too. It helps to make the stocks in advance. That way, you can refrigerate them and remove any fat that rises to the surface before using. Most soups thicken as they sit. If you plan to make soup ahead or store leftovers, have extra stock on hand to thin the soup when you reheat it. Save the stock in a special place until you're ready to use it—just make sure your special place is refrigerated. Stock will keep up to 1 week in the fridge. Not having stock when you need it is like not having cash at the checkout counter. It's an empty feeling.

EQUIPMENT

It is important to choose the right pot for cooking soups. A *stockpot* is a high-walled pot that is taller than it is wide. It's ideal for long, slow simmering, and the reduced surface area inhibits evaporation in soups such as minestrone, split pea, lentil, and tomato basil. A *rondeau* is a two-handled pot that is wider than it is tall. It's great for soups that call for browning meat (such as beef ribs, and lamb shanks), because the increased surface area reduces crowding and ingredients sauté rather than steam. We never use aluminum pots for our soups because they react chemically with acidic ingredients, such as tomatoes and wine, and this reaction produces a metallic taste.

NECESSARY UTENSILS

- **LIDS,** to prevent evaporation.
- **SPOONS,** for skimming fat and tasting.
- **SLOTTED SPOONS,** for stirring without creating a whirlpool.
- **KNIVES,** the duller, the more dangerous.
- **CUTTING BOARD,** keep it clean.
- **LADLES,** for serving.
- **HANDS,** for whenever tools don't work.
- **FINGERS,** for whenever hands don't work.
- **TONGUE,** if the soup doesn't touch your tongue often enough, it's unloved.

WORKING WITH FRESH HERBS AND SPICES

We like to use the stems of herbs, like rosemary, thyme, and cilantro, to season our soups. Just tie the stems together with a piece of string, cook as directed, and remove the stems before serving (cilantro stems are tender enough to stay in the pot). Some fresh herbs are too delicate to be added to soup at the beginning. Chervil, tarragon, basil, cilantro leaves, chives, and mint are added to soup at the end or used as a garnish. Rosemary, parsley, thyme, sage, lemongrass, Kaffir lime leaves, oregano, and bay leaves can withstand long cooking times, and they actually taste better when given a chance to stew for awhile.

The stems and roots of dill and tarragon are usually discarded along with chicken bones, but when chopped and added to soup, they impart a surprising fragrance and extra dose of flavor.

Dried herbs, such as rosemary, bay leaves, and thyme are added early in soup cooking because as they cook, the dried leaves and seeds perfume the broth without overpowering it. Avoid dried basil, oregano, sage, tarragon, and parsley—the dried versions of these fresh herbs are too strong, and they don't taste anything like their fresh counterparts.

WHAT WE MEAN WHEN WE SAY . . .

"Chicken, cut up"

Almost all of our soups with chicken call for it cut up. You can have your butcher do it, you can purchase one already cut up, or you can buy a whole chicken and cut it into eight pieces yourself—cut each breast in half and cut away the two legs, two thighs and two wings.

"Chopped"

In our soups, that means to cut into very large chunks. Our vegetables are typically chopped into two-inch pieces, making our soups thick and hearty, with lots of large pieces floating around. When we want you to slice something differently, we tell you (i.e., thinly sliced; cut into ¼-inch cubes; cut julienne).

"Cook beans until tender"

Cook until beans are tender but not mushy. The best way to tell if a bean is tender is to taste it—or you can squeeze one between two fingers to see if it's soft.

"Cook potatoes until tender"

This means fork tender—when potatoes fall off a fork when pierced—not when they break apart. In some soups, we cook the potatoes until they break up, using the starch to add body and thickness to the broth.

"Heat through"

We often use this term at the end of cooking, when a few last minute ingredients have been added. This means to warm the new ingredients, not to cook for any length of time.

"Lightly toasted"

We often toast ingredients like nuts and shredded coconut before adding them to soup (toasting yields a more nutty flavor). To toast, spread nuts or coconut on a baking sheet and bake in a 350 degree oven for 5 minutes, shaking the pan occasionally to promote even browning. After toasting, nuts and coconut should be golden in color, not dark brown.

"Sauté"

To cook in a small amount of fat until golden brown and tender. The time to reach a golden brown surface varies depending on the ingredients used.

"Simmer until liquid is reduced"

Simmer until about half of the liquid has cooked off, or evaporated. This intensifies the flavor, like orange juice concentrate.

"Stir to coat"

Usually called for after herbs and spices have been added to the pot. Coating vegetables and meat ensures that all the herbs and spices are distributed evenly throughout the soup.

"Sweat vegetables until tender"

Sweating means to soften without browning (unlike sautéing, which means to tenderize and brown), and it usually takes about 5 minutes over medium heat. When vegetables are tender, as with onions, celery, and fennel, it means that they're pliable and wilted, but not mushy.

Hi. I read a review and saw something on TV about Daily Soup. When my wife and I visited New York City from Memphis, we were pleasantly surprised to find a Daily Soup shop right around the corner from our hotel. We ordered soup and immediately wondered when Daily Soup would be leaving New York and finding a home in the South—preferably Memphis? Yummy :-)) Thanks for making a great trip even better and best of luck—though you don't need it—for the future.

VEGETABLE

THE FIVE MOST frequently used vegetables in our soups are onions, carrots, celery, leeks, and garlic. There are other varieties, but the Big 5 are the most versatile, adaptable, and durable.

Seasonality is extremely important when cooking with vegetables. Although most vegetables are available year-round, they're not always at their peak, and flavor and texture can be compromised. For example, the taste and texture of leeks, tomatoes, mushrooms, peppers, okra, figs, and asparagus vary greatly throughout the year. And, in the winter months, leeks have a hard core, or "piece of wood," that significantly reduces the edible portion of the vegetable.

There are four ways to use vegetables in soup:

1. use them to enhance flavor;
2. use them to dominate flavor;
3. puree them to create a thick broth;
4. poach them to create a rich stock.

Most people think vegetable soups and stocks have less flavor than meat-based soups and stocks. Not true. It all depends on how the vegetables are cooked. This is the challenge of vegetable cooking. You must strive to get the maximum flavor from vegetables, and the cooking technique greatly affects the outcome. Roasting, grilling, caramelizing, and poaching all produce different flavors, and these flavors are infused into the broth. To get the most flavor from your vegetable, remember, you're the boss and the vegetable must know it. Although we assume vegetables "get the point" as soon as they see the knife.

A vegetable soup is deemed "good" when a nonvegetarian craves it. That's the ultimate compliment. We serve a lot of vegetarian customers at Daily Soup. Whether for ethical, moral, political, or health reasons, the number of vegetarians in the United States has nearly doubled in the past decade.

Vegetables "throw" water when they cook. The water content in some vegetables is staggering—lettuce and other leafy greens can be as much as 90 percent water, celery about 70 percent, and beets around 50 percent. When vegetables cook, they shrink in size, sometimes drastically, and they add liquid to the soup or stock. For a thick vegetable soup, you must add a tremendous amount of raw ingredients.

We like to use grilled and roasted vegetables in our soups. Sometimes grilled and roasted vegetables have an overpowering flavor because the "charred" flavor takes over and the inherent taste of the vegetable is lost. In fact, they taste like the grill and not like the vegetable. But, when those same grilled and roasted vegetables are added to soup, the grilled taste spreads out, the vegetable flavor is resurrected, and the broth takes on a delicate, smoky flavor.

Most vegetables work well with cream, yogurt, milk, and cheese. And, not only do dairy products add a rich and creamy balance, they help spread flavors across the palate.

CREAMLESS ASPARAGUS

2	tablespoons canola oil
1	large Spanish onion, chopped
2	celery stalks, chopped
2	carrots, peeled and chopped
3	teaspoons kosher salt
2	teaspoons dried thyme leaves
2	bay leaves
2	teaspoons mustard seeds

¼	teaspoon ground white pepper
6	cups Basic Vegetable Stock (page 223)
1	medium potato, peeled and grated
2	pounds fresh asparagus, stems peeled and sliced into ½-inch thick rounds, tips set aside
1	teaspoon minced fresh garlic
2	tablespoons chopped fresh dill

COOK'S NOTE: We love the fact that fresh asparagus and mustard seeds have a natural affinity for one another. The intense flavor of mustard complements asparagus while bringing out the vegetable's fresh taste.

1. Heat the oil in a large stockpot over medium heat. Add the onion, celery, and carrots and sweat 4 minutes, until tender.

2. Add the salt, thyme, bay leaves, mustard seeds, and pepper and stir to coat the vegetables.

3. Add stock, potato, and asparagus rounds and bring the mixture to a boil. Reduce heat, partially cover and simmer for 30 minutes.

4. Remove bay leaves, puree half of the soup in a blender or food processor, and return puree to the pot.

5. Add the asparagus tips and simmer 4 minutes.

6. Remove from heat and stir in the garlic.

7. To serve, ladle the soup into bowls and garnish with the fresh dill.

MAKES 10 CUPS.

FRENCH ONION

VARIATION:

FRENCH ONION SOUP WITH CHICKEN Substitute Blonde Chicken Stock (page 226) for the Basic Vegetable Stock. Poach 1 pound boneless, skinless chicken breasts in gently simmering water for 10 minutes. Drain and, when cool enough to handle, cut into 2-inch cubes. Add to the soup at step 6 and proceed as directed.

1	tablespoon peanut oil		½	teaspoon ground black pepper
1	tablespoon unsalted butter		1	cup Tawny Port
3	large Spanish onions, halved and thinly sliced		8	cups Basic Vegetable Stock (page 223)
3	large red onions, halved and thinly sliced		1	(3-inch) piece Parmesan cheese rind
1	tablespoon sugar		¼	cup grated Parmesan cheese
2	teaspoons dried thyme leaves		1	tablespoon balsamic vinegar
2	bay leaves		1	teaspoon minced fresh garlic
2	teaspoons kosher salt		1	sourdough baguette, cut crosswise into 1-inch rounds and lightly toasted
			2	cups grated Gruyere cheese

1. Preheat the oven to 400 degrees.
2. Combine the oil, butter, onions, and sugar in a large roasting pan. Place in the oven and roast for 1 hour, stirring every 15 minutes, until the onions are tender and golden brown.
3. Transfer the onions to a large stockpot over medium heat.
4. Add the thyme, bay leaves, salt, and pepper and stir to coat the onions.
5. Add the port and simmer until the liquid is absorbed.
6. Add the stock and Parmesan rind and bring the mixture to a boil.
7. Reduce heat, partially cover, and simmer 30 minutes.
8. Stir in the grated Parmesan, balsamic vinegar, and garlic.
9. Preheat the broiler.
10. Remove the bay leaves and ladle the soup into bowls.
11. Top each bowl with a sourdough round.
12. Top with the grated Gruyere cheese and place under the broiler. Broil until the cheese is golden and bubbly, about 3 minutes.

MAKES 10 CUPS.

MINESTRONE WITH PESTO

2 tablespoons olive oil

1 large Spanish onion, chopped

2 celery stalks, chopped

2 leeks, rinsed well and chopped

2 garlic cloves, minced

2 teaspoons dried thyme leaves

2 bay leaves

2 teaspoons kosher salt

½ teaspoon ground black pepper

½ pound cannellini or navy beans, rinsed and picked over to remove debris

8 cups Basic Vegetable Stock (page 223)

1 (28-ounce) can whole tomatoes, drained and diced

2 cups cauliflower flowerets

½ cup fresh fava beans, shelled, or frozen lima beans, thawed

1 zucchini, halved lengthwise and sliced

1 yellow squash, halved lengthwise and sliced

1 bunch escarole, chopped

1 cup Basil Pesto (page 237)

½ cup chopped scallions

1. Heat the oil in a large stockpot over medium heat. Add the onion, celery, leeks, and garlic and sweat for 4 minutes, until tender.

2. Add the thyme, bay leaves, salt, and pepper and stir to coat the vegetables.

3. Add the cannellini beans, stock, and tomatoes and bring the mixture to a boil. Reduce heat, partially cover, and simmer 1 to 2 hours, until the beans are tender.

4. Add the cauliflower, fava beans, zucchini, and yellow squash and simmer 5 minutes.

5. Remove from heat, stir in the escarole and pesto, cover, and let steep for 1 minute.

6. To serve, remove the bay leaves, ladle the soup into bowls and top with the chopped scallions.

MAKES 12 CUPS.

COOK'S NOTE:
For this soup, we like to make the pesto separately and stir it in at the end. We've borrowed this technique from Italian cooks who rely on pesto to add a fresh basil taste to richly flavored soups.

TIP:
Make extra pesto to use in salad dressings or as a spread on sandwiches and toasted sourdough bread.

WILD MUSHROOM ARTICHOKE

VARIATION:

WILD MUSHROOM WITH POTATOES AND GREENS
Add 4 quartered red bliss potatoes with the artichoke and mushroom stock (step 6) and simmer for 15 minutes. Stir in 1 bunch of fresh chopped kale instead of artichoke hearts (step 7). Remove from the heat and stir in the balsamic vinegar.

8   baby artichokes (golf-ball size), stems and tops trimmed, tough outer leaves removed (if baby artichokes are not available, substitute water-packed artichoke hearts)

8   cups Basic Vegetable Stock (page 223)

½   cup vermouth

1   tablespoon olive oil

1   tablespoon fresh lemon juice

4   teaspoons dried thyme leaves

4   bay leaves

4   tablespoons unsalted butter

2½ pounds mushrooms (any mixed variety of button, shiitake, oyster, cremini, chanterelles, and black trumpet), stems removed and reserved, caps sliced

8   cups mineral or filtered water

½   cup white port or white wine

3   medium white onions, chopped

2   celery stalks, chopped

2   leeks, rinsed well and chopped

2   garlic cloves, minced

2   teaspoons dried rosemary

2   teaspoons kosher salt

½   teaspoon ground black pepper

1   tablespoon balsamic vinegar

1. Combine the artichokes, stock, vermouth, olive oil, lemon juice, 2 teaspoons of the thyme, and 2 bay leaves in a large stockpot over medium heat. Bring to a boil, reduce heat, and simmer for 15 minutes, until the artichokes are tender. Remove the artichokes with a slotted spoon and reserve 4 cups of stock. When the artichokes are cool enough to handle, cut them into quarters and set aside.

2. Melt 2 tablespoons of the butter in a large stockpot over medium heat. Add the mushroom stems and a few cremini or button mushrooms and sweat for 5 minutes, until tender and releasing juice. Add the water and white port and bring the mixture to a boil. Reduce the heat, partially cover, and simmer for 20 minutes.

Strain the stock through a fine sieve to remove solids, reserving 4 cups of liquid, and set aside.

3. Melt the remaining 2 tablespoons of butter in a large stockpot over medium heat. Add the onions, celery, leeks, and garlic and sweat for 4 minutes, until tender.

4. Add the remaining 2 teaspoons of thyme and 2 bay leaves, the rosemary, salt, and pepper and stir to coat the vegetables.

5. Add the sliced mushroom caps and sauté for 5 minutes.

6. Add the reserved artichoke and mushroom stock and bring the mixture to a boil. Reduce heat, partially cover, and simmer for 15 minutes.

7. Stir in the reserved artichoke hearts and simmer for 5 minutes.

8. Remove from the heat and stir in the balsamic vinegar.

9. To serve, remove the bay leaves and ladle the soup into bowls.

MAKES 10 CUPS.

WINTER MINESTRONE

2 tablespoons olive oil

1 large Spanish onion, chopped

2 garlic cloves, minced

½ head cabbage, preferably Savoy, chopped

2 teaspoons dried thyme leaves

1 bunch fresh basil stems (leaves removed), tied together with string

1½ teaspoons kosher salt

½ teaspoon ground black pepper

8 cups Basic Vegetable Stock (page 223)

1 butternut squash (about 1½ pounds), peeled, seeded, and cut into 1-inch cubes

4 red bliss potatoes, cut into 1-inch cubes

3 tablespoons tomato paste

1 (3-inch) piece Parmesan cheese rind

2 cups uncooked spinach radiatore pasta, or any spiral pasta

1 cup Basil Pesto (page 237)

½ cup chopped scallions

1. Heat the oil in a large stockpot over medium heat. Add the onion and garlic and sweat for 4 minutes, until tender.

2. Add the cabbage and sweat for 4 minutes, until wilted.

3. Add the thyme, basil stems, salt, and pepper and stir to coat the vegetables.

4. Add the stock, squash, potatoes, tomato paste, and Parmesan rind and bring the mixture to a boil. Reduce heat, partially cover, and simmer for 10 minutes.

5. Add the pasta and cook for 10 minutes, until tender.

6. To serve, remove the basil stems and Parmesan rind, ladle the soup into bowls, and top with a dollop of pesto and the chopped scallions.

MAKES 10 CUPS.

JAMAICAN PUMPKIN

2 tablespoons peanut oil	¼ teaspoon ground allspice
1 large Spanish onion, chopped	¼ teaspoon ground nutmeg
2 celery stalks, chopped	2 white yams or potatoes, peeled, halved
2 garlic cloves, minced	lengthwise, and cut into 1-inch cubes
1 tablespoon minced fresh ginger	4 cups cubed calabaza or fresh pumpkin
1 tablespoon sugar	6 cups Basic Vegetable Stock (page 223)
2 teaspoons kosher salt	1 teaspoon Pickapeppa sauce (optional)
1 teaspoon turmeric	½ cup chopped scallions

COOK'S NOTE:
Calabaza is a round Jamaican pumpkin, usually about 5 pounds, and available in gourmet markets. Treat it as you would a regular pumpkin or any winter squash.

1. Heat the oil in a large stockpot over medium heat. Add the onion, celery, garlic, ginger, and sugar and sweat for 4 minutes, until tender.

2. Add the salt, turmeric, allspice, and nutmeg and stir to coat the vegetables.

3. Add the yams, calabaza, and stock and bring the mixture to a boil.

4. Reduce heat, partially cover, and simmer for 20 minutes, until the yams and calabaza are tender.

5. Puree half of the soup in a blender or food processor and return to the pan. Remove from the heat and stir in the Pickapeppa sauce.

6. To serve, ladle the soup into bowls and top with the chopped scallions.

MAKES 10 CUPS.

GRILLED VEGETABLES WITH FETA CHEESE

4	tablespoons olive oil
1	medium eggplant (about 1 pound), halved lengthwise
2	red bell peppers, halved and seeded
4	scallions, ends trimmed and halved
1	zucchini, halved lengthwise
1	yellow squash, halved lengthwise
1	cup fresh green beans, ends trimmed
1	large Spanish onion, chopped
2	celery stalks, chopped
2	garlic cloves, thinly sliced

2	teaspoons dried thyme leaves
2	teaspoons dried oregano
2	bay leaves
2	teaspoons kosher salt
½	teaspoon ground cinnamon
½	teaspoon ground black pepper
6	cups Basic Vegetable Stock (page 223)
1	(28-ounce) can whole tomatoes, drained and diced
½	cup crumbled feta cheese

1. Preheat an outdoor grill or stove-top grill pan.

2. In a large bowl, combine 2 tablespoons of the oil, the eggplant, red peppers, scallions, zucchini, yellow squash, and green beans and toss to coat the vegetables.

3. Place the vegetables on the grill and cook for 4 minutes, until tender crisp and slightly charred with grill marks on all sides. Remove from the grill and when cool enough to handle, cut into 1-inch pieces; set aside.

4. Heat the remaining 2 tablespoons of oil in a large stockpot over medium heat. Add the onion, celery, and garlic and sweat for 4 minutes, until tender.

5. Add the thyme, oregano, bay leaves, salt, cinnamon, and pepper and stir to coat the vegetables.

6. Add the stock and tomatoes and bring the mixture to a boil. Reduce heat, partially cover, and simmer for 20 minutes.

7. Add the grilled vegetables and simmer 2 minutes.

8. To serve, remove the bay leaves, ladle the soup into bowls, and top with the feta cheese.

MAKES 12 CUPS.

ROASTED EGGPLANT PARMESAN

3   medium eggplant (about 1 pound each), halved

3   large beefsteak tomatoes, cut into 1-inch cubes

2   tablespoons unsalted butter

1   large Spanish onion, chopped

2   celery stalks, chopped

3   garlic cloves, minced

2   teaspoons dried thyme leaves

2   bay leaves

2   teaspoons kosher salt

¼   teaspoon cayenne

6   cups Basic Vegetable Stock (page 223)

1   (28-ounce) can whole tomatoes, drained and diced

1   (3-inch) piece Parmesan cheese rind

¼   cup grated Parmesan cheese

½   cup chopped fresh basil

COOK'S NOTE:

This is the soup equivalent to one of our favorite Italian dishes—eggplant parmesan. Serve it with a nice chunk of sourdough bread to soak up the broth.

1. Preheat the oven to 400 degrees.

2. Cut one eggplant into 1-inch cubes. Spread the eggplant cubes, 2 eggplant halves and beefsteak tomatoes on a baking sheet coated with nonstick spray. Roast in the oven for 30 minutes, turning once during cooking. Remove from the oven and when cool enough to handle, core the eggplant halves, puree the center, and cut the remaining shell into 1-inch cubes; set aside.

3. Melt the butter in a large stockpot over medium heat. Add the onion, celery, and 2 of the garlic cloves and sweat for 4 minutes, until tender.

4. Add the thyme, bay leaves, salt, and cayenne and stir to coat the vegetables.

5. Add the roasted eggplant cubes, roasted beefsteak tomatoes, eggplant puree, stock, canned tomatoes, and Parmesan rind and bring the mixture to a boil. Reduce heat, partially cover, and simmer for 20 minutes.

6. Remove from heat and stir in the grated Parmesan, basil, and remaining garlic clove.

7. To serve, remove the bay leaves and Parmesan rind, and ladle the soup into bowls.

MAKES 10 CUPS.

ROASTED RED PEPPER

6	red bell peppers	¼	teaspoon cayenne
2	tablespoons unsalted butter	6	cups Basic Vegetable Stock (page 223)
1	large Spanish onion, chopped	1	bunch basil, stems tied together, leaves chopped
2	celery stalks, chopped		
2	teaspoons dried thyme leaves	1	cup heavy cream
2	bay leaves	3	garlic cloves
2	teaspoons kosher salt		

1. Preheat the broiler.

2. Place the red peppers under the broiler, 4 inches from the heat source, and char on all sides (or roast peppers over the flame of a gas burner). When blackened on all sides, remove from the broiler and place in a paper bag for 5 minutes to steam. Remove them from the bag, peel the charred skin, halve, seed, and chop into ½-inch pieces; set aside.

3. Heat the butter in a large stockpot over medium heat. Add the onion and celery and sweat for 4 minutes, until tender.

4. Add the thyme, bay leaves, salt, and cayenne and stir to coat the vegetables.

5. Add ½ of the chopped red peppers, the stock, and basil stems and bring the mixture to a boil. Reduce heat, partially cover, and simmer for 20 minutes.

6. Meanwhile, combine the heavy cream and garlic in a small saucepan over medium heat. Simmer until the cream is reduced by half.

7. Transfer the garlic cream to a blender, add the remaining roasted red peppers, and puree until smooth.

8. Place the puree in a pot, stir, and heat through.

9. Remove from the heat and stir in the basil leaves.

10. To serve, remove the bay leaves and basil stems and ladle the soup into bowls.

MAKES 10 CUPS.

VEGETARIAN • DAIRY FREE • LOW FAT

BORSCHT

Our first next-door neighbor was a suit tailor named Murray Bittman. Murray is an old-school New Yorker. Almost every day he said, "When are you gonna make borscht???" "What's a soup place without borscht?" "It will fly out the door," "You know what you gotta do? Put fresh beets in there," "Make it kosher." Here is your Borscht, Murray.

10 fresh beets, peeled and grated
4 tablespoons sugar
2 tablespoons peanut oil
8 cups mineral or filtered water
1 large Spanish onion, peeled
2 garlic cloves, minced
1 (28-ounce) can whole tomatoes, drained and diced

2½ teaspoons kosher salt
½ teaspoon ground black pepper
2 eggs, whisked slightly
1 cucumber, halved, seeded, and cut into ¼-inch pieces
2 tablespoons fresh lemon juice
2 tablespoons grated fresh horseradish
½ cup chopped scallions

DERMATOLOGIST'S NOTE: *Borscht* is an old Slavic word for beet, the vegetable that gives this soup its characteristic red color. Beets also impart their beautiful color to your hands—so wear gloves when peeling and chopping.

1. Preheat the oven to 425 degrees.
2. In a large roasting pan, combine the grated beets, sugar, and oil. Stir to coat the beets. Place in the oven and roast for 45 minutes, stirring occasionally. Remove them from the oven and transfer to a large stockpot.
3. Add the water, whole onion, garlic, tomatoes, salt, and pepper. Bring the mixture to a boil, reduce heat, partially cover, and simmer for 20 minutes.
4. Remove the onion with a slotted spoon.
5. Reduce heat to low and gradually add the eggs, whisking constantly, until the soup thickens (whisking constantly prevents the eggs from curdling and forming lumps).
6. Stir in the cucumber, lemon juice, and grated horseradish.
7. Refrigerate until ready to serve.
8. To serve, ladle the borscht into bowls and top with the chopped scallions.

MAKES 12 CUPS.

31

WINTER BORSCHT WITH BEEF SHORT RIBS

4 tablespoons peanut oil	2 celery stalks, chopped
3 pounds beef short ribs on the bone, cut up	2 carrots, peeled and chopped
	2 garlic cloves, minced
10 cups Blonde Chicken Stock (page 226), or mineral water	2 teaspoons dried thyme leaves
	2 bay leaves
10 fresh beets, peeled	2 red bliss potatoes, cut into 1-inch cubes
2 tablespoons sugar	
1 tablespoon unsalted butter, cut into small dice	1 tablespoon grated fresh horseradish
	1 tablespoon fresh lemon juice
1 large Spanish onion, chopped	½ cup sour cream
1 head Savoy cabbage, cored and sliced	½ cup chopped chives
2 teaspoons kosher salt	

1. Preheat the oven to 425 degrees.

2. Heat 2 tablespoons of the oil in a large stockpot over medium heat. Add the beef short ribs and brown on all sides. Add the chicken stock and bring the mixture to a boil. Reduce heat, partially cover, and simmer for 45 minutes. Remove the beef ribs with a slotted spoon, reserving the stock, and when cool enough to handle, pull the meat from the bones and set aside. Strain the stock to remove solids, remove surface oil, and reserve 6 cups.

3. Meanwhile, coarsely grate 3 of the beets and cut the remaining 7 into 1-inch cubes. Spread all the beets out in a roasting pan and sprinkle with sugar and diced butter. Place in the oven and roast for 45 minutes, turning occasionally. Remove from the oven and set aside.

4. Heat the remaining 2 tablespoons of oil in a large stockpot over medium heat. Add the onion, cabbage, and salt and sweat for 4 minutes.

5. Add the celery, carrots, and garlic and sweat for 2 minutes.

6. Add the thyme and bay leaves and stir to coat the vegetables.

7. Add the reserved beef, roasted beets, beef stock, and potatoes and bring the mixture to a boil. Reduce heat, partially cover, and simmer for 20 minutes.

8. Stir in the horseradish and lemon juice.

9. To serve, remove the bay leaves, ladle the borscht into bowls, and top with the sour cream and chives.

MAKES 12 CUPS.

CUCUMBER WITH YOGURT AND CILANTRO

VARIATION:

CUCUMBER YOGURT WITH DILL

Substitute fresh dill for the cilantro. Eliminate the cumin and serve with fresh chopped chives.

4	cucumbers	2	cups plain yogurt
1	tablespoon fresh lemon juice	1	cup heavy cream
2	garlic cloves	½	cup chopped fresh cilantro
2	tablespoons sugar	2	cups Basic Vegetable Stock (page 223), or mineral water
2½	teaspoons kosher salt		
2	teaspoons ground cumin seeds	½	cup thinly sliced red onion
¼	teaspoon cayenne	½	cup chopped scallions

1. Peel 2 of the cucumbers, remove and reserve seeds, and cut into small triangles. Cut the remaining cucumbers in half, remove and reserve the seeds, and cut into small dice.
2. Puree the cucumber seeds in a blender with the lemon juice, garlic, sugar, salt, cumin, and cayenne.
3. Add the yogurt, heavy cream, and cilantro and process until blended.
4. Transfer to a large bowl and stir in the reserved cucumbers, stock, and red onion.
5. Refrigerate until ready to serve.
6. To serve, ladle the soup into bowls and top with the chopped scallions.

MAKES 12 CUPS.

CAULIFLOWER VICHYSSOISE

2 tablespoons unsalted butter

2 leeks, rinsed well and chopped

2 teaspoons dried thyme leaves

2 bay leaves

2½ teaspoons kosher salt

½ teaspoon ground black pepper

¼ teaspoon ground nutmeg

4 heads fresh cauliflower, flowerets removed, about 8 to 10 cups cauliflower flowerets

10 cups Basic Vegetable Stock (page 223), or mineral water

2 cups heavy cream

½ cup chopped fresh Italian parsley

VARIATION:
CREAM OF CAULIFLOWER
Serve hot with chopped scallions.

1. Melt the butter in a large stockpot over medium heat. Add the leeks and sweat for 4 minutes, until tender.

2. Add the thyme, bay leaves, salt, pepper, and nutmeg and stir to coat the leeks.

3. Add half of the cauliflower flowerets and the stock and bring to a boil. Reduce heat, partially cover, and simmer for 20 minutes, until tender.

4. Meanwhile, blanch the remaining cauliflower flowerets in a large pot of rapidly boiling, lightly salted water for 2 minutes. Drain, rinse under cold water to prevent further cooking, and set aside.

5. Remove the bay leaves from the soup and stir in the heavy cream.

6. Using a hand blender or food processor, puree the soup until smooth.

7. Transfer the mixture to a large bowl and stir in the blanched cauliflower.

8. Refrigerate until ready to serve.

9. To serve, ladle the soup into bowls and top with the chopped parsley.

MAKES 12 CUPS.

TOMATO

TOMATOES EVOKE STRONG feelings in people. While some crave a fresh, ripe, summer tomato, others can't stand the sight of them (they even pick them out of salads). *Those* people call them "fruit," and they're the same people who love ketchup and frozen pizza. But, the tomato doesn't mind. The tomato knows it will be eaten in some form. The tomato is passive. It's patient. It doesn't need to play hard to get because everyone eventually comes around. Those skeptics will eventually learn what the rest of us have known for years—the tomato is good.

Our apologies to those who are allergic to tomatoes, you may skip this chapter.

The flavor of a tomato varies greatly depending on seasonality, ripeness, and the region where it was grown. In soup, the riper the tomato, the sweeter and richer the outcome. Plum tomatoes are great, as are very ripe Jersey or beefsteak tomatoes. The hydroponic tomatoes may look deep red and ripe, but they're flavorless. Some recipes call for a specific variety (i.e., beefsteak tomatoes in the Roasted Eggplant Parmesan, page 29, or plum tomatoes in the Tomato Basil, page 39), meaning that's the best variety for that dish. Unless specified, any ripe tomato variety will work in our soups.

When we develop soup, it's hard to keep tomatoes out of it. We put tomatoes in chilis, Indian soups, South and Central American soups, African soups, Italian, French, bean, lentil, cheese, grain, Eastern European, Cajun, Spanish, and even Asian soups. They're everywhere! They're like chameleons, changing color and taste, depending on which soup they're in. For those tomato loathers, watch out! They are everywhere, you just can't see them.

We use tomatoes in various ways—raw (Gazpacho, page 43), roasted (Eggplant Parmesan, page 29), stewed (all of our Indian soups), and sautéed (Crawfish Étouffée, page 197). A lot of our customers buy extra-large containers of Tomato Basil (page 39) to use as pasta sauce. We don't consider that odd. You can take a bath in our Tomato Basil if you like. As long as you're enjoying yourself.

A WORD ABOUT CANNED TOMATOES

There's no better canned fruit or vegetable than the canned tomato, especially the peeled, whole plum tomatoes imported from Italy. They're quickly boiled, peeled, and canned, and they lose none of their sweet taste and nutritional value. The acidity level of canned tomatoes varies from can to can, and you must cook off the acid flavor to prevent the soup from tasting raw.

A NOTE ABOUT STORING TOMATOES

Always store fresh tomatoes at room temperature—refrigeration kills flavor.

TOMATO BASIL

One night, we were about to close the shop, when a group of women came in. They wanted our Tomato-Roasted Garlic. They bought it all—everything we had. After they emptied the pots, they went to our freezer and bought all the frozen Tomato-Roasted Garlic. They scoured every nook and cranny of the store for the soup. Turns out, they were throwing an impromptu singles party and wanted to use our soup as a pasta sauce. (We recommended Granny Smith apples for dessert, to neutralize the garlic breath.)

2	tablespoons unsalted butter	6	cups Basic Vegetable Stock (page 223)
1	large Spanish onion, chopped	1	(28-ounce) can whole tomatoes, diced
2	leeks, rinsed well and chopped	2	cups heavy cream
2	celery stalks, chopped	1	tablespoon brandy
1	tablespoon sugar	4	Italian plum tomatoes, seeded and diced
2	teaspoons dried thyme leaves		
2	bay leaves	¾	cup basil pesto (page 237)
2	teaspoons kosher salt	1	teaspoon minced fresh garlic
½	teaspoon ground black pepper	½	cup chopped fresh chives
⅛	teaspoon cayenne		

1. Melt the butter in a large stockpot over medium heat. Add the onion, leeks, celery, and sugar and sauté for 10 minutes, until caramelized and golden brown.
2. Add the thyme, bay leaves, salt, pepper, and cayenne and stir to coat the vegetables.
3. Add the stock and canned tomatoes, bring the mixture to a boil, reduce heat, partially cover, and simmer for 30 minutes.
4. Stir in heavy cream and brandy and simmer 2 minutes.

VARIATION:

TOMATO FENNEL
Add one chopped fennel bulb to the onion, leek, celery, and sugar mixture (step 1). Sweat the vegetables as directed. Add 1 teaspoon whole fennel seeds with the addition of the thyme, bay leaves, salt, black pepper, and cayenne (step 2). Proceed with the recipe as directed.

VARIATION:

TOMATO-ROASTED GARLIC
Preheat oven to 450°. Wrap 2 whole heads of garlic in foil and roast in oven for 15 minutes, until tender. When cool enough to handle, remove cloves from skin and puree in a food processor or blender; set aside. Meanwhile, combine the 2 cups heavy

cream, brandy and 4
fresh garlic cloves in
a medium sauce pan.
Simmer 20 minutes,
until garlic is tender
and cream is reduced
by half. Remove from
heat and puree in a
food processor or
blender until smooth.
Follow the above
recipe as directed
until after the 30
minute simmering
time. When directed to
add heavy cream and
brandy, stir in roasted
garlic and garlic
cream. Proceed with
the remainder of the
recipe as directed.

5. Remove the bay leaves and puree about half of the soup in a blender or food processor until smooth.

6. Return the puree to the pot stir in the basil pesto, and heat through.

7. Remove from the heat and stir in the plum tomatoes and garlic.

8. To serve, ladle the bisque into bowls and top with the chopped chives.

MAKES 12 CUPS.

TOMATO, BASIL, AND MOZZARELLA

6	beefsteak tomatoes (about 4 pounds), halved and seeded, seeds reserved	½	cup fresh basil leaves, cut into very fine strips
2	tablespoons olive oil	½	pound fresh boconccini mozzarella (about 20 1-inch balls), thinly sliced, or regular mozzarella cut into 1-inch cubes
2	garlic cloves		
1	tablespoon balsamic vinegar		
2	teaspoons kosher salt		
½	teaspoon ground black pepper	½	cup chopped scallions
2	cups tomato juice		

1. In a blender or food processor, combine half of the tomatoes and all of the tomato seeds, olive oil, and garlic. Puree until smooth. Add the vinegar, salt, and pepper and process until blended.
2. Chop the remaining tomatoes into small dice.
3. Transfer the pureed mixture to a large bowl and stir in the chopped tomatoes, tomato juice, basil, and mozzarella.
4. Refrigerate until ready to serve.
5. To serve, ladle the soup into bowls and top with the chopped scallions.

MAKES 12 CUPS.

GREEK TOMATO WITH TRAHANA PASTA

COOK'S NOTE:

In Greece, this soup is also made with orzo, or tiny rice-shaped pasta. We make it with Trahana, which is a Greek pasta made with sour milk and shaped into little pebbles. Couscous can be substituted for the pasta if desired. This soup is a specialty on the island of Mykonos.

2 tablespoons olive oil
3 medium white onions, chopped
2 garlic cloves, minced
1 tablespoon sugar
2 teaspoons ground cumin seeds
2 teaspoons dried oregano
2 teaspoons kosher salt
½ teaspoon ground black pepper
¼ teaspoon ground cinnamon

1 (28-ounce) can whole tomatoes, diced
8 cups Basic Vegetable Stock (page 223)
2 ripe beefsteak tomatoes, seeded and diced
1 cup uncooked trahana pasta or couscous
½ cup crumbled feta cheese
½ cup chopped scallions

1. Heat the oil in a large stockpot over medium heat. Add the onion, garlic, and sugar and sweat for 4 minutes, until tender.
2. Add the cumin, oregano, salt, pepper, and cinnamon and stir to coat.
3. Add the canned tomatoes and simmer for 5 minutes.
4. Add the stock, bring the mixture to a boil, reduce heat, partially cover, and simmer for 20 minutes.
5. Stir in the fresh tomatoes, pasta, and 2 tablespoons of the feta cheese; simmer for 2 minutes.
6. Remove from the heat and let stand 5 minutes.
7. To serve, ladle the soup into bowls and top with the remaining feta cheese and chopped scallions.

MAKES 12 CUPS.

GAZPACHO

2	red bell peppers	2	garlic cloves
2	green bell peppers	1	Pickled Jalapeño (page 237)
2	yellow bell peppers	2	teaspoons kosher salt
2	beefsteak tomatoes, stems removed and tomatoes halved	1	teaspoon habañero chile, or other hot sauce
4	cups tomato juice	2	cucumbers, halved, seeded, and cut into ¼-inch cubes
2	tablespoons olive oil		
2	tablespoons red wine vinegar	½	cup chopped fresh cilantro
1	tablespoon sherry vinegar	½	cup chopped scallions

1. Halve the peppers, remove the seeds and white portion, and transfer the seeds and white portion (the items normally discarded in other recipes!) to a blender or food processor.

2. Add the tomatoes, 2 cups of the tomato juice, oil, both vinegars, garlic, jalapeño, salt, and hot sauce and puree until smooth.

3. Transfer the mixture to a large bowl and add the remaining tomato juice.

4. Cut the peppers (flesh portion) into small dice.

5. Stir the diced peppers, cucumber, and cilantro into the pureed mixture.

6. Refrigerate until ready to serve.

7. To serve, ladle the soup into bowls and top with the chopped scallions.

MAKES 12 CUPS.

SHRIMP AND SCALLOP SEVICHE

½ pound medium shrimp, peeled and deveined

½ pound scallops

6 beefsteak tomatoes (about 4 pounds), halved and seeded, seeds reserved

1 cup Basic Vegetable Stock (page 223)

1 Pickled Jalapeño (page 237)

2 garlic cloves

2 tablespoons fresh lemon juice

2½ teaspoons kosher salt

1 cup tomato juice

½ cup chopped fresh cilantro

½ cup thinly sliced red onion

½ cup chopped fresh parsley

1. Cook the shrimp and scallops in a large pot of rapidly boiling water for 3 minutes, until the shrimp are bright red and cooked through. Rinse under cold water to prevent further cooking and set aside.

2. Cut half of the tomatoes into small dice and set aside.

3. In a blender or food processor, combine the remaining tomatoes, all of the tomato seeds, stock, jalapeño, garlic, lemon juice, and salt. Puree until smooth.

4. Transfer the pureed mixture to a large bowl and stir in the diced tomatoes, shrimp and scallops, tomato juice, cilantro, and red onion.

5. To serve, ladle the soup into bowls and top with the chopped parsley.

MAKES 12 CUPS.

Dear Daily Soup,

My boss was sick so I bought him some of your Chicken Rice. I got a raise!!

Dear Daily Soup,

This is an emergency . . . I need your recipe for Pea Parmesan Soup. I poured it into a plastic cup and told my sister that I made it. She doubts I can cook and I need to prove to her I can. She wants me to make it for Christmas. Do you give out your recipes? This is a dire situation. If you can't send it to me, please send me something that makes it sound like I know what I'm talking about. Please, please, please!!!

Just wondering . . .

Has your cookbook come out yet? Also, will it have soups for picky preschoolers?

Daily Soupers,

We've been having an office debate . . . do you use the same recipe for the white, black, and red bean chilis? I think the white bean tastes the best and the red bean is thicker. We have a pool to determine which one you will run next. Go white bean.

RICE

MOST OF THE world subsists on rice. In fact, many cultures consider a meal incomplete when rice is not on the plate or in the bowl. There are over 7,000 varieties of rice grown in the world today. For those who have trouble making decisions, you'll be happy to know that only a handful are available in the United States. And, at Daily Soup, we narrowed that field even further to a chosen few. Initially, we tried to use Basmati and Japanese sushi rice in some of our soups, but they didn't perform as well as regular white or Arborio rice.

Rice is typically an easy grain to cook, but it doesn't always cooperate in soup. One of the best properties of rice, and what makes it ideal for soup, is its ability to absorb broth and soak up flavor. But, rice doesn't know when to stop absorbing. It will eventually mop up every last bit of broth or explode if it's cooked too long. That's why we add rice late in the cooking process, when we can make sure there's plenty of liquid available in which the rice can expand.

The cooking time for rice must be long enough to completely cook the rice, but not so long that it dehydrates the soup. So, if you come back to the kitchen and there's no soup in the pot—just a giant piece of rice—you waited too long.

Sometimes we cook rice separately and add it to soup just before serving, eliminating the risk of a brothless soup, or the revenge of the giant rice kernel.

CHICKEN AND SEAFOOD JAMBALAYA

COOK'S NOTE:
We've learned that the trick to perfect jambalaya is taking . . . our . . . time. No need to rush this dish. Make this soup in a series of steps for the most wonderful meal you've ever had.

2 links (about ¾ pound) andouille sausage

10 cups mineral or filtered water

4 tablespoons peanut oil

1 whole chicken (about 4 pounds), cut up (see page 13)

1 large Spanish onion, chopped

2 celery stalks, chopped

2 green bell peppers, seeded and chopped

1 red bell pepper, seeded and chopped

¼ pound tasso ham (see Ingredient Index, page 240), diced, or smoked ham

2 teaspoons dried thyme leaves

2 teaspoons dried oregano

2 bay leaves

1½ teaspoons onion powder

1½ teaspoons garlic powder

1½ teaspoons mustard powder

½ teaspoon cayenne

½ teaspoon ground black pepper

½ teaspoon ground white pepper

½ teaspoon kosher salt

2 (28-ounce) cans whole tomatoes, drained and diced

6 cups Basic Shellfish Stock (page 225)

1 cup uncooked white rice

1 pound medium shrimp, peeled and deveined

1 pound lobster meat

½ cup chopped scallions

1. Combine the sausage and 5 cups of the water in a medium saucepan over medium heat. Bring to a boil, reduce heat, and poach for 10 minutes. Remove the sausage with a slotted spoon and reserve 2 cups of liquid. When the sausage is cool enough to handle, slice into rounds and set aside.

2. Heat 2 tablespoons of the oil in a large stockpot over medium heat. Add the chicken pieces and brown on all sides. Add the remaining 5 cups of water, bring to a boil, reduce heat, and simmer for 10 minutes, until the chicken is cooked through. Remove the chicken from the pot and reserve the broth for another use. When the chicken is cool enough to handle, pull the meat from the bones and set aside (discard bones).

3. Heat the remaining 2 tablespoons of oil in the stockpot and add the onion, celery, green and red peppers, and ham. Sweat for 4 minutes, until tender.

4. Add the thyme, oregano, bay leaves, the onion, garlic and mustard powders, the cayenne, the black and white peppers, and the salt. Stir to coat the vegetables.

5. Add the tomatoes, shellfish stock, reserved sausage poaching liquid, reserved chicken, and sliced andouille sausage.

6. Bring to a boil, reduce heat, partially cover, and simmer for 10 minutes.

7. Add the rice and simmer for 15 minutes.

8. Stir in the shrimp and lobster. Simmer for 3 minutes, until the shrimp are bright red and cooked through.

9. To serve, remove the bay leaves, ladle the jambalaya into shallow bowls, and top with the chopped scallions.

MAKES 12 CUPS.

VALENCIAN-STYLE PAELLA

1   pound chorizo (about 4 links)

18 cups mineral or filtered water

6   baby artichokes (golf-ball size), ends and tops trimmed, tough outer leaves removed (if baby artichokes are not available, substitute water-packed artichoke hearts)

1   teaspoon dried thyme leaves

1   tablespoon fresh lemon juice

5   tablespoons olive oil

1   whole chicken (about 4 pounds), cut up (see page 14)

1   large Spanish onion, chopped

2   red bell peppers, seeded and chopped

3   garlic cloves, minced

15 saffron threads

2   teaspoons dried rosemary

2   bay leaves

2   teaspoons kosher salt

1   cup uncooked Spanish short-grain rice, or Arborio rice

1   (28-ounce) can whole tomatoes, drained and diced

2   tablespoons tomato paste

1   pound medium shrimp, peeled and deveined

½   pound cooked lobster meat, cut into 1-inch pieces

1   cup shelled fresh green peas

½   cup chopped fresh Italian parsley

1. Combine the chorizo and 5 cups of the water in a large stockpot over medium heat. Bring to a boil, reduce heat, and poach for 10 minutes. Remove the chorizo with a slotted spoon and reserve 2 cups of liquid. When cool enough to handle, slice the chorizo into thin rounds and set aside.

2. Meanwhile, combine the artichokes, 5 cups of water, thyme, lemon juice, and 1 tablespoon of the oil in a medium saucepan over medium heat. Bring to a boil, reduce heat, partially cover, and simmer for 15 minutes, until the artichokes are tender. Remove the artichokes with a slotted spoon and reserve the stock, and when cool enough to handle, quarter the artichokes and set aside. Strain the stock to remove solids, reserving 2 cups, and set aside.

3. Heat 2 tablespoons of the oil in a large stockpot over medium heat. Add the chicken pieces and brown on all sides. Add 8 cups of water, bring to a boil,

reduce the heat, and simmer for 10 minutes, until the chicken is cooked through. Remove the chicken with a slotted spoon, and when cool enough to handle remove the meat from bones and set aside. Strain poaching liquid to remove solids, reserving 2 cups, and set aside.*

4. Heat the remaining 2 tablespoons of oil in a large stockpot over medium heat. Add the onion, red peppers, and garlic and sweat for 4 minutes, until tender.

5. Add the saffron, rosemary, bay leaves, and salt and stir to coat the vegetables.

6. Add the tomatoes and tomato paste and simmer for 10 minutes.

7. Add the rice and sauté until golden, stirring constantly.

8. Add the reserved chorizo and artichoke poaching liquids.

9. Add the chicken and chicken poaching liquid, partially cover, and simmer for 15 minutes, stirring frequently.

10. Stir in the shrimp, lobster, peas, and reserved chorizo and artichokes. Simmer for 3 minutes, until the shrimp are bright red and cooked through.

11. To serve, remove the bay leaves, ladle the paella into bowls, and top with the chopped parsley.

MAKES 12 CUPS.

*To de-fat the stock, refrigerate for 1 hour, until a fat layer forms on the surface. Skim the layer of fat off the top and discard.

YUCATAN CHICKEN-LIME

COOK'S NOTE:

*Found in Mexican specialty stores and gourmet markets (see Ingredient Index, page 240).

4 tablespoons peanut oil

1 whole chicken (about 4 pounds), cut up (see page 14)

10 cups mineral or filtered water

3 medium white onions, chopped

2 green bell peppers, seeded and chopped

2 garlic cloves, minced

½ avocado leaf*

1 teaspoon dried, ground epazote*

1 dried chipotle pepper, minced*

1 chipotle chile in adobo with ½ teaspoon sauce, minced*

2½ teaspoons kosher salt

½ cup uncooked white rice

½ cup chopped scallions

½ cup chopped fresh cilantro

¼ cup fresh lime juice

2 cups corn tortilla chips

1. Heat 2 tablespoons of the oil in a large stockpot over medium heat. Add the chicken pieces and brown on all sides. Add the water, bring to a boil, reduce heat and simmer for 10 minutes, until the chicken is cooked through. Remove the chicken with a slotted spoon and reserve the poaching liquid. When cool enough to handle, remove the meat from the bones and set aside. Strain the poaching liquid to remove solids, reserving 8 cups, and set aside.

2. Heat the remaining 2 tablespoons of oil in a large stockpot over medium heat. Add the onions, bell peppers, and garlic and sweat for 4 minutes, until tender.

3. Add the avocado leaf, epazote, dried chipotle, chipotle in adobo with sauce, and salt and stir to coat the vegetables.

4. Return the chicken and reserved poaching liquid to the pot, bring to a boil, reduce heat, partially cover, and simmer for 20 minutes.

5. Add the rice and simmer for 20 minutes, until tender.

6. Remove from heat, stir in the scallions, cilantro, and lime juice, cover, and let steep for 1 minute.

7. To serve, remove the avocado leaf, ladle the soup into bowls, and garnish with the corn chips.

MAKES 10 CUPS.

A SOUP BY ANY OTHER NAME IS STILL A SOUP

BISQUE: A cream-based fish or seafood soup. Because the seafood is simmered in stock over low heat, the result is a rich broth with moist and tender chunks of fish and seafood. It is also a fun word to say.

BORSCHT: A robust Russian stew made with beets, tomatoes, cabbage, and, oftentimes, meat.

BOUILLABAISSE: A classic Provençal fisherman's stew made with a mixture of fish and shellfish, garlic, tomatoes, saffron, and fennel.

CHOWDER: The word "chowder" comes from the French Chaudière, a type of cauldron used to cook soup for large gatherings. The early American settlers made chowder with household staples, things like salt pork, local fish, sea biscuits, and bread. In the nineteenth century, potatoes replaced the crackers and milk or cream was added for their rich flavor and wonderful thickening properties. Hence, the origin of the milk-based chowder. Obviously, we've taken chowders to yet another level.

ÉTOUFFÉE (É too fay): The process of cooking pork, poultry, or seafood in a small amount of liquid (similar to braising) and then smothering the meat with aromatic vegetables. The pot is then covered and the whole thing is allowed to cook until the flavor from the vegetables transcends into the meat. This is an excellent way to ensure flavor and moisture in any type of meat, poultry, or seafood dish.

GAZPACHO: A pureed mixture of summery vegetables, including fresh tomatoes, cucumber, and onion. Classic versions of Gazpacho are often thickened with bread, but it's not essential to the success of the soup.

GUMBO: *Quingombo* is the African Congo word for okra—that's how the term "gumbo" came to be known as the infamous, thick Louisiana soup, one that's thickened with okra or ground sassafras root (filé powder).

JAMBALAYA: A New Orleans–style dish (one that resembles a pilaf) usually made with some combination of rice, pork, ham, chicken, shrimp, and a variety of herbs and spices.

MINESTRONE: A classic vegetable and bean soup from Italy. Cooks frequently add fresh, seasonal produce, pasta, cheese, and pesto to create unlimited variations.

MULLIGATAWNY: There are countless variations of this Indian soup, but almost all involve curried meat or seafood that's smothered in cream or coconut milk.

PAELLA: The word "paella" comes from the "paella pan," a broad, shallow pan traditionally used to cook this classic dish from Spain. The original paella was made with rice, chicken, rabbit, beans, and sometimes snails. Cooks from all over the globe have since added a variety of ingredients, such as fish, shellfish, vegetables, pork, and sausage.

POSOLE: A traditional Latin American stew served on special occasions and "feast days." A hearty blend of chile peppers, vegetables, hominy, and stock.

POTAGE: The most variable of all soups, a potage is typically the "special of the day," meaning one prepared with the freshest seasonal ingredients.

POT PIE: A mixture of chicken or turkey and mixed vegetables in a thick cream sauce, topped with a flaky pastry crust.

SEVICHE: Fresh, raw seafood (usually grouper, halibut, flounder, and snapper), marinated in an acid, such as tomato or lemon juice. The acid in the marinade "cooks" the fish, removing any raw taste, and the result is a flavorful dish with tender chunks of seafood.

STEW: The browning of small pieces of meat, poultry, or fish, then simmering them with vegetables or other ingredients in enough liquid to cover all the ingredients. Stews are usually cooked in a closed or partly closed stockpot or Dutch oven, either on top of the stove or in the oven.

VICHYSSOISE: A classic French soup made with potatoes, leeks, stock, and heavy cream or milk. The mixture is typically pureed, garnished with fresh chives, and served chilled.

GRAIN, PASTA, AND BREAD

AN AGE OLD soup ritual involves crumbling crackers and dried bread into soup. No one knows who started this ceremony or where it started, but somehow it became popular. One thing we do know—this practice makes it difficult to keep the tablecloth clean.

Actually, crackers and bread act as sponges by soaking up the broth and rounding out almost any soup. Pasta, matzoh balls, dumplings, rice, and whole grains serve the same function when added to soup, but when you use those, you don't have messy cracker wrappers to clean up.

With grains, cooking times vary depending on the density of the kernel. Barley, wheatberries, and farro take longer to cook than rice or pasta, so they're added early in the cooking process. Quinoa, couscous, and bulgur cook very quickly, so they're added near the end. With pasta, it's virtually impossible to obtain an "al dente" texture in soup, so just let go, you can't control it.

Couscous is actually pasta made from durum semolina. To make couscous, semolina granules are rolled in water and then lightly coated with flour to form tiny pellets. *Trahana* is a Greek pasta made a similar way, but sour milk or yogurt is used instead of water (Greek Tomato with Trahana Pasta, page 42).

Barley is known for its chewy texture and wheatlike, nutty flavor. Wild Mushroom Barley (page 62) is a staple in every Jewish and Polish kitchen, and

59

Budweiser (also made from barley) is a staple at every sporting event and bachelor party.

Quinoa ("keen-wa") is a fast-cooking grain that becomes almost translucent when cooked. It's got a subtle, nutty flavor and can be used in recipes that call for bulgur or rice.

Italian farro or *spelt* is a mild-flavored grain from Tuscany, similar to barley, wheatberries, and bulgur. We often use it to add body and thickness to our soups.

In Italy, unsalted bread is simmered in a hot, garlic-tomato sauce until it's mushy and then the mixture is topped with olive oil, Parmigiano-Reggiano, and basil. It's called Papa al Pommodoro, and the bread breaks down to the texture of oatmeal. In fact, if you didn't know it was bread, you would guess it was polenta. We recreated this dish in our Tuscan Bread (page 70) and Chicken Garlic Bread (page 68) soups.

The grain movement of the late 1960s culminated in the rescue of thousands of starving Woodstock concert-goers. Organizers of the event seriously underestimated the size of the crowd and the food quickly ran out. The roads were jammed with people and cars trying to get to the concert, and there was no way to bring in additional food. The only way to get supplies to the delirious crowd was to drop it from planes and helicopters. So, organizers dropped barrels of couscous and soy sauce into makeshift kitchens and volunteers quickly mixed the couscous with water and served it with the soy sauce. Wavy Gravy called it "Breakfast in Bed for four hundred thousand people."

FARRO AND CHICKPEAS

1   ounce dried porcini or shiitake
     mushrooms
2   cups warm mineral or filtered water
2   tablespoons olive oil
1   large Spanish onion, chopped
2   garlic cloves, minced
1   bunch fresh rosemary, leaves chopped,
     stems reserved
2   bay leaves
2   teaspoons kosher salt

½   pound dried chickpeas (garbanzo
     beans), rinsed and drained
6   cups Basic Vegetable Stock (page
     223), or mineral water
1   (28-ounce) can whole tomatoes,
     drained and diced
1   cup Italian farro (spelt)
1   cup shelled fava beans, or frozen lima
     beans, thawed
½   cup grated Parmesan cheese

1. Combine the porcini mushrooms and warm water and set aside for 20 minutes.
   Strain the porcinis through a paper towel–lined sieve, reserving the liquid.
   Chop and set aside.

2. Heat the oil in a large stockpot over medium heat. Add the onion and garlic and
   sweat for 4 minutes, until tender.

3. Tie the rosemary stems together and add to the pot with the bay leaves and salt.
   Stir to coat the vegetables.

4. Add the chickpeas, porcinis, porcini soaking liquid, stock, tomatoes, and farro.
   Bring to a boil, reduce heat, partially cover, and simmer for 1 hour, until the
   farro is tender.

5. Stir in the fava beans, Parmesan, and chopped rosemary and simmer for 2 minutes.

6. To serve, remove the rosemary stems and bay leaves and ladle the soup into
   bowls.

MAKES 10 CUPS.

VEGETARIAN · DAIRY FREE · LOW FAT

WILD MUSHROOM BARLEY

VARIATION:

WILD MUSHROOM BAR-
LEY WITH CHICKEN
Poach 1 pound bone-
less, skinless chicken
breasts in gently sim-
mering water for 10
minutes. Drain and
when cool enough to
handle, cut into 2-inch
cubes. Add the chicken
to the soup at the end
of the cooking time
(step 6) and simmer
for 2 minutes to heat
through. Remove from
the heat and stir in the
parsley, vinegar, and
garlic (step 7).

- 4 tablespoons olive oil
- 2½ pounds mushrooms (any mixed variety of button, shiitake, oyster, cremini, chanterelles, and black trumpet), stems removed and reserved, caps sliced
- 10 cups mineral or filtered water
- ½ cup white port, or white wine
- 1 large Spanish onion, chopped
- 2 celery stalks, chopped
- 2 carrots, peeled and chopped
- 2 teaspoons dried thyme leaves
- 2 bay leaves
- 2 teaspoons kosher salt
- ½ teaspoon black pepper
- 1 cup uncooked pearl barley
- ½ cup chopped fresh Italian parsley
- 1 tablespoon balsamic vinegar
- 1 teaspoon minced fresh garlic

1. Heat 2 tablespoons of the olive oil in a large stockpot over medium heat. Add the mushroom stems and a few cremini or button mushroom caps and sweat for 5 minutes, until tender and releasing juice.
2. Add the water and port and bring the mixture to a boil. Reduce heat, partially cover, and simmer for 20 minutes. Strain the stock through a fine sieve to remove solids, reserving 8 cups of liquid; set aside.
3. Place the pot over medium heat and heat the remaining 2 tablespoons olive oil. Add the onion, celery, and carrots and sweat for 4 minutes, until tender.
4. Add the thyme, bay leaves, salt, and pepper and stir to coat the vegetables.
5. Add the sliced mushroom caps and sauté for 5 minutes, until tender and releasing juice.
6. Add the reserved mushroom stock and pearl barley. Bring to a boil, reduce heat, and simmer for 1 hour, until the barley is tender.
7. Remove from heat and stir in the parsley, vinegar, and garlic.
8. To serve, remove the bay leaves and ladle the soup into bowls.

MAKES 12 CUPS.

CHICKEN BARLEY SOUP

2	tablespoons peanut oil		2	bay leaves
2	pounds skinless, boneless chicken (thighs and breasts), cut into 2-inch cubes		1	teaspoon kosher salt
			½	teaspoon ground black pepper
1	large Spanish onion, chopped		8	cups Blonde Chicken Stock (page 226)
2	celery stalks, chopped		1	cup uncooked pearl barley
2	carrots, peeled and chopped		⅓	cup dry vermouth
2	teaspoons dried thyme leaves		¼	cup chopped fresh Italian parsley

1. Heat the oil in a large stockpot over medium heat. Add the chicken pieces and brown on all sides. Remove the chicken from the pan with a slotted spoon, reserving the oil in the pan, and set aside.

2. Add the onion, celery, and carrots to the pan and sweat for 4 minutes, until tender.

3. Add the thyme, bay leaves, salt, and pepper and stir to coat the vegetables.

4. Return the chicken to the pan and add the stock and pearl barley. Bring to a boil, reduce heat, partially cover, and simmer for 1 hour, until the barley is tender.

5. Stir in the vermouth and simmer for 2 minutes to heat through.

6. To serve, remove the bay leaves, ladle the soup into bowls, and top with the chopped parsley.

MAKES 12 CUPS.

VARIATION:

BEEF BARLEY
Sauté 3 pounds of beef short ribs in 2 tablespoons of vegetable oil until browned on all sides. Add 10 cups of mineral or filtered water and bring to a boil. Reduce heat, partially cover, and simmer for 45 minutes. Remove the beef ribs with a slotted spoon, reserving the stock, and when cool enough to handle, pull the meat from the bones and set aside. Strain the stock to remove solids, remove surface oil, and reserve 8 cups. Proceed as directed to Step 4. Return the beef and stock to the pan and stir in the pearl barley. Continue with the recipe.

MOROCCAN CHICKEN CURRY
WITH COUSCOUS

4	tablespoons peanut oil
1	whole chicken (about 4 pounds), cut up (see page 14)
10	cups mineral or filtered water
1	large Spanish onion, chopped
2	red bell peppers, seeded and chopped
2	celery stalks, chopped
2	garlic cloves, minced
1	tablespoon minced fresh ginger
1	tablespoon sugar
2	teaspoons kosher salt
2	teaspoons ground curry
1½	teaspoons ground coriander seeds

1	teaspoon turmeric
½	teaspoon ground black pepper
¼	teaspoon ground cinnamon
1	butternut squash (about 1½ pounds), peeled, seeded, and cut into 1-inch cubes
1	zucchini, halved lengthwise and cut into 1-inch cubes
1	cup shelled fresh fava beans, or frozen lima beans, thawed
½	cup uncooked couscous
1	bunch fresh kale, chopped
½	cup chopped fresh cilantro

1. Heat 2 tablespoons of the oil in a large stockpot over medium heat. Add the chicken pieces and brown on all sides. Add the water, bring to a boil, reduce heat, and simmer for 10 minutes, until the chicken is cooked through. Remove the chicken with a slotted spoon, reserve the poaching liquid, and when cool enough to handle remove the meat from the bones and set aside. Strain the poaching liquid to remove solids, reserving 8 cups, and set aside.*

2. Heat the remaining 2 tablespoons of the oil in the pot over medium heat. Add the onion, bell peppers, celery, garlic, and ginger and sweat for 4 minutes, until tender.

*To de-fat the stock, refrigerate for 1 hour, until a fat layer forms on the surface. Skim the layer of fat off the top and discard.

3. Add the sugar, salt, curry, coriander, turmeric, pepper, and cinnamon and stir to coat the vegetables.

4. Add the chicken, reserved poaching liquid, and butternut squash. Bring the mixture to a boil, reduce heat, partially cover, and simmer for 15 minutes.

5. Stir in the zucchini, fava beans, and couscous, cover, and simmer for 2 minutes.

6. Remove from the heat, stir in the kale, cover, and let stand for 5 minutes.

7. To serve, ladle the soup into bowls and top with chopped cilantro.

MAKES 12 CUPS.

CHICKEN MATZOH BALL

When we were developing soup recipes, Chicken Matzoh Ball was, by far, the fiercest argument we had. Imagine this—three Jews gesturing and debating around a table to determine who makes the "best" matzoh ball soup. Should they be floaters or sinkers? Small or large? Should they have cinnamon or ginger? Should the matzoh meal be precooked or raw? It's like politics and religion; it can get very ugly. We tried all three variations on our customers, and medium-size "sinkers" were the winner.

4	tablespoons canola oil
1	whole chicken (about 4 pounds), cut up (see page 14)
10	cups mineral or filtered water
1	large Spanish onion, chopped
2	celery stalks, chopped
3	carrots, peeled and chopped
1	bunch fresh thyme, leaves chopped and stems reserved
2	bay leaves
2	teaspoons kosher salt
½	teaspoon ground black pepper
2	cups fresh shelled green peas
½	cup dry vermouth
1	teaspoon minced fresh garlic
½	cup chopped fresh Italian parsley

REGINA'S MATZOH BALLS:

2½	cups mineral or filtered water
¾	cup schmaltz (chicken fat), or vegetable oil
1½	teaspoons kosher salt
2½	cups matzoh meal
1½	teaspoons chopped fresh Italian parsley
½	teaspoon ground ginger
7	eggs

1. Heat 2 tablespoons of the oil in a large stockpot over medium heat. Add the chicken pieces and brown on all sides. Add the water, bring to a boil, reduce heat, and simmer for 10 minutes, until the chicken is cooked through. Remove the chicken with a slotted spoon, reserve the poaching liquid, and when cool

enough to handle remove the meat from the bones and set aside. Strain the poaching liquid to remove solids, reserving 8 cups, and set aside.*

2. Heat the remaining 2 tablespoons of oil in the pot over medium heat. Add the onion, celery, and carrots and sweat for 4 minutes, until tender.

3. Tie the thyme stems together and add them to the pot with the bay leaves, salt, and pepper.

4. Add the chicken and reserved poaching liquid and bring the mixture to a boil. Reduce heat, partially cover, and simmer for 20 minutes.

5. Meanwhile, to make the matzoh balls, combine the water, schmaltz, and salt in a medium saucepan over medium heat and bring to a boil.

6. Gradually add the matzoh meal and stir with a wire whisk until the mixture pulls away from the sides of the pan.

7. Stir in the parsley and ginger and mix well.

8. Add the eggs, one at a time, mixing well after each addition. Reduce heat to low and cook for 25 minutes, stirring frequently.

9. Drop the matzoh dough by heaping spoonfuls into the simmering soup.

10. Cover and simmer 15 minutes.

11. Stir in the chopped thyme, vermouth, and garlic and heat through.

12. To serve, remove the bay leaves and thyme stems, ladle the soup into bowls, and top with the chopped parsley.

MAKES 12 CUPS.

*To de-fat the stock, refrigerate for 1 hour, until a fat layer forms on the surface. Skim the layer of fat off the top and discard.

CHICKEN GARLIC BREAD

1   sourdough baguette (about ½ pound and preferably day-old), cut into 1-inch cubes
5   tablespoons olive oil
1   teaspoon garlic powder
2½ teaspoons kosher salt
1   whole chicken (about 4 pounds), cut up (see page 14)
8   cups mineral or filtered water
1   large Spanish onion, chopped
2   celery stalks, chopped

2   leeks, rinsed well and chopped
2   garlic cloves, thinly sliced
2   teaspoons dried thyme leaves
2   bay leaves
½   teaspoon ground black pepper
1   (28-ounce) can whole tomatoes, drained and diced
1   (3-inch) piece Parmesan cheese rind
½   cup shaved Parmesan (shave block of Parmesan with vegetable peeler)

1. Preheat the oven to 300 degrees.

2. In a large bowl, combine the bread cubes, 1 tablespoon of the olive oil, garlic powder, and ½ teaspoon of salt and toss to coat the bread. Spread the bread cubes out on a baking sheet, place in the oven, and bake for 40 minutes, until crisp all the way through. Remove from the oven and set aside until ready to use.

3. Heat 2 tablespoons of the oil in a large stockpot over medium heat. Add the chicken pieces and brown on all sides. Add the water, bring to a boil, reduce heat, and simmer 10 minutes, until the chicken is cooked through. Remove the chicken with a slotted spoon, reserve the poaching liquid, and when cool enough to handle remove the meat from the bones and set aside. Strain the poaching liquid to remove solids, reserving 6 cups, and set aside.*

*To de-fat the stock, refrigerate for 1 hour, until a fat layer forms on the surface. Skim the layer of fat off the top and discard.

4. Heat the remaining 2 tablespoons of the oil in a large stockpot over medium heat. Add the onion, celery, leeks, and garlic cloves and sweat for 4 minutes, until tender.

5. Add the thyme, bay leaves, remaining 2 teaspoons of salt, and pepper and stir to coat the vegetables.

6. Add the reserved chicken stock, chicken meat, tomatoes, and Parmesan rind and bring the mixture to a boil. Reduce heat, partially cover, and simmer for 20 minutes.

7. Remove the bay leaves and Parmesan rind with a slotted spoon.

8. Remove the soup from the heat and stir in the bread cubes. Let stand 5 minutes.

9. To serve, ladle the soup into bowls and garnish with the shaved Parmesan.

MAKES 12 CUPS.

TUSCAN BREAD SOUP

1	sourdough baguette (about ½ pound and preferably day-old), cut into 1-inch cubes	½	teaspoon ground black pepper
3	tablespoons olive oil	⅛	teaspoon cayenne
1	teaspoon garlic powder	6	cups Basic Vegetable Stock (page 223)
2½	teaspoons kosher salt	1	(28-ounce) can whole tomatoes, drained and diced
1	large Spanish onion, chopped	1	bunch basil stems, tied together
2	celery stalks, chopped	½	cup shaved Parmesan cheese (shave block of Parmesan with vegetable peeler)
2	leeks, rinsed well and chopped		
2	garlic cloves, thinly sliced	½	cup chopped fresh Italian parsley
2	teaspoons dried thyme leaves		

1. Preheat the oven to 300 degrees.
2. In a large bowl, combine the bread cubes, 1 tablespoon of the olive oil, garlic powder, and ½ teaspoon of salt and toss to coat bread. Spread the bread cubes out on a baking sheet, place in the oven, and bake for 40 minutes, until crisp all the way through. Remove from the oven and set aside until ready to use.
3. Heat the remaining 2 tablespoons of the oil in a large stockpot over medium heat. Add the onion, celery, leeks, and garlic cloves and sweat for 4 minutes, until tender.
4. Add the thyme, remaining 2 teaspoons of salt, pepper, and cayenne and stir to coat the vegetables.
5. Add the stock, tomatoes, and basil stems and bring the mixture to a boil. Reduce the heat, partially cover, and simmer for 20 minutes.
6. Remove from the heat, remove the basil stems, and stir in the toasted bread cubes. Let stand for 5 minutes.
7. To serve, ladle the soup into bowls and garnish with the shaved Parmesan and chopped parsley.

MAKES 12 CUPS.

Overheard on the New York City subway:

Four boys were critiquing girls as they got on and off the train. Finally one of the boys said "Yo, that's a Daily Soup bone" motioning to a young woman. We don't know what that means, but word of mouth comes in all forms.

I relocated from New York to Los Angeles and miss your soup more than anything—more than Rockefeller Center at Christmas, more than exhaust fumes and pigeons. Is it possible to get frozen soup shipped to LA?

CORN

UNLIKE RICE OR potatoes, which are neutral and take on the flavor of other ingredients, corn has a distinct flavor that will always *win* when added to soup. Yellow or white, corn has a sweet and obvious flavor that can overwhelm soup if it's not added in the proper balance with other ingredients.

We rely on corn stock to ensure that our soups have depth. Boiling the cobs in vegetable stock, chicken stock, shellfish stock, or milk extracts the full, sweet flavor of the corn, and guarantees that you won't dump any of that flavor in the trash.

We use different forms of corn in our soups. Because of its high starch content, pureed corn is used to thicken soup. Hominy, used in Posole (page 84), is dried corn (with the hull and germ removed) soaked in wood ash lye or lime. What's the hull and what's the germ? We don't know, but hominy kernels are huge because the soaking process increases their size. They're bigger than hazelnuts! Once cooked, hominy is soft, much like a chickpea, and very different in texture from regular corn. Grits are broken hominy grains.

Corn meal is a corn derivative used to make corn tortillas and polenta. Ever heard of the Italian food pop quiz? Here it is: "How long do you cook polenta?" That's the first question every accomplished Italian cook asks. This is a test. The answer? "Forty-five minutes." Say that, and you will be revered forever. "Al dente" is just a tease.

Corn tortilla chips (Mexican bread) are added to all of our Mexican soups. Tortillas are added at the end of cooking to impart a subtle corn taste and additional layer of flavor. Fried tortillas are tastier, but the baked varieties can be substituted to keep the overall fat content down.

CHICKEN SUCCOTASH

4	tablespoons unsalted butter	2	teaspoons kosher salt
1	whole chicken (about 4 pounds), cut up (see page 14)	½	teaspoon ground black pepper
8	cups mineral or filtered water	1	cup heavy cream
8	ears fresh corn, kernels sliced from cob, about 4 cups	3	garlic cloves
		2	cups frozen lima beans, thawed
1	large Spanish onion, chopped	12	patty pans (golf ball-size), halved lengthwise, or 1 zucchini, halved lengthwise and sliced
2	celery stalks, chopped		
2	teaspoons dried thyme leaves	4	plum tomatoes, seeded and chopped
2	bay leaves		

(see page 14)

COOK'S NOTE:

Succotash refers to the combination of corn and lima beans, a mixture introduced to the early American settlers by the North American Indians.

1. Melt 2 tablespoons of the butter in a large stockpot over medium heat. Add the chicken pieces and brown on all sides. Add the water, bring to a boil, reduce heat, and simmer for 10 minutes, until the chicken is cooked through. Remove the chicken with a slotted spoon, reserve the poaching liquid, and when cool enough to handle remove the meat from the bones and set aside. Strain the poaching liquid to remove solids, reserving 6 cups, and set aside.*

2. Puree about 1 cup of the corn in a blender or food processor and set aside.

3. Melt the remaining 2 tablespoons of butter in the pot over medium heat. Add the onion and celery and sweat for 4 minutes, until tender.

4. Add the thyme, bay leaves, salt, and pepper and stir to coat the vegetables.

5. Add the chicken, reserved poaching liquid, pureed corn, and whole corn kernels. Bring the mixture to a boil, reduce heat, partially cover, and simmer for 10 minutes.

*To de-fat the stock, refrigerate for 1 hour, until a fat layer forms on the surface. Skim the layer of fat off the top and discard.

75

6. Meanwhile, combine the heavy cream and garlic in a small saucepan over medium heat. Simmer until the cream reduces by half. Puree the cream mixture in a blender until smooth; set aside.

7. Add the lima beans and patty pans to the chicken mixture and simmer for 5 minutes.

8. Stir in the pureed heavy cream and tomatoes and simmer for 1 minute.

9. To serve, remove the bay leaves and ladle the soup into bowls.

MAKES 12 CUPS.

CORN, RED PEPPER, AND ZUCCHINI CHOWDER

8   ears fresh corn, kernels sliced from
    cob and cobs reserved, about 4 cups
8   cups Basic Vegetable stock (page 223)
2   tablespoons unsalted butter
1   large Spanish onion, chopped
2   celery stalks, chopped
2   ramps,* or leeks, rinsed well and
    chopped
2   red bell peppers, seeded and chopped
2   teaspoons dried thyme leaves

2   bay leaves
2   teaspoons kosher salt
¼   teaspoon cayenne
6   medium Idaho potatoes, peeled, halved
    lengthwise, and cut into 1-inch cubes
1   zucchini, halved lengthwise and sliced
½   cup heavy cream
1   teaspoon minced fresh garlic
1   bunch fresh chives, sliced into ¾-inch
    strips

COOK'S NOTE:

To get *layers* of flavor, we use every part of each ingredient. For this recipe, we use corn cobs to make a rich stock first, and then we use the stock to enhance the corn flavor of the chowder.

* Ramps are members of the onion family and resemble scallions or leeks. Chop up the flavorful green leaves and add them to the chowder.

1. Combine the corn cobs and stock in a large stockpot over medium heat. Bring to a boil, reduce heat, partially cover, and simmer for 30 minutes. Remove the cobs with a slotted spoon and discard. Reserve 6 cups of the stock and set aside.

2. Melt the butter in a large stockpot over medium heat. Add the onion, celery, ramps, and red pepper and sweat for 4 minutes, until tender.

3. Add the thyme, bay leaves, salt, and cayenne and stir to coat the vegetables.

4. Add the corn, potatoes, and reserved stock and bring the mixture to a boil. Reduce the heat, partially cover, and simmer for 30 minutes.

5. Add the zucchini and simmer for 5 minutes.

6. Stir in the heavy cream.

7. Remove the bay leaves and puree about one quarter of the chowder in a blender or food processor until smooth.

8. Return the puree to the pot and mix well.

9. Remove from the heat and stir in the fresh garlic.

10. To serve, ladle the chowder into bowls and top with sliced chives.

MAKES 12 CUPS.

MEXICAN TORTILLA SOUP

VARIATION:

MEXICAN TORTILLA
SOUP WITH CHICKEN
Poach 1 pound bone-
less, skinless chicken
breasts in gently sim-
mering water for 10
minutes. Drain and
when cool enough to
handle, cut into 2-inch
cubes. Add to the soup
after step 4. Simmer
for 2 minutes to heat
through. Pick up at
step 5 and proceed
with the recipe as
directed.

4   cups plus 2 tablespoons peanut oil
12 corn tortillas, cut into bite-size pieces
2½ teaspoons kosher salt
4   medium white onions, chopped
2   garlic cloves, minced
2   teaspoons dried Mexican oregano (see
    Ingredient Index, page 240), or regular
    dried oregano
1   bunch cilantro stems, thinly sliced
1   chipotle chile in adobo, with ½
    teaspoon sauce, minced*

1   (28-ounce) can whole tomatoes,
    drained and diced
6   cups Basic Vegetable Stock (page 223)
½   cup chopped scallions
½   cup chopped fresh cilantro
2   tablespoons fresh lime juice
1   teaspoon minced fresh garlic
½   cup grated Queso Blanco* or Monterey
    Jack cheese
1   Haas avocado,** peeled, seeded, and
    cubed

1. Heat all but 2 tablespoons of the oil in a large stockpot over medium heat until
   it reaches 380 to 400 degrees. Add the corn tortillas in batches and fry until
   golden brown. Remove the tortilla chips with a slotted spoon, place on paper
   toweling to drain, and sprinkle with 1 teaspoon of salt. Discard the frying oil or
   reserve for another use.

2. Heat the remaining 2 tablespoons of oil in a large stockpot over medium heat.
   Add the onions and garlic and sweat for 4 minutes, until tender.

3. Add the oregano, cilantro stems, and remaining 1½ teaspoons of salt and stir to
   coat the vegetables.

*Available in Mexican specialty stores and gourmet markets.

**We like to use Haas avocados, the purplish-black variety from California. Because Haas avocados contain
twice as much fat as the smaller, smooth-skin green avocados from Florida, they have a rich and buttery
flesh that is perfectly suited for our soups.

4. Stir in the chipotle and chipotle sauce, tomatoes, and stock, bring to a boil, reduce heat, partially cover, and simmer for 30 minutes.

5. Stir in one handful of the fried tortillas, scallions, cilantro, lime juice, and garlic and simmer for 2 minutes to heat through.

6. To serve, place the fried tortillas in the bottom of bowls, ladle the soup over the top, sprinkle grated cheese on top, and garnish with the avocado.

MAKES 10 CUPS.

POBLANO CORN CHOWDER

VARIATION:

CRAB CORN CHOWDER
Eliminate the poblano
chilies from the
recipe. Stir in 1 pound
of lump crabmeat after
pureeing one quarter
of the chowder (step
6). Proceed with the
recipe as directed.

VARIATION:

DIVER SCALLOP CORN
CHOWDER
Add 1 pound shucked
Diver scallops after
pureeing one quarter
of the chowder (step
6). Simmer 3 minutes,
until the scallops are
cooked through. Pro-
ceed with the recipe
as directed.

8 ears fresh corn, kernels sliced from
cob and cobs reserved, about 4 cups

10 cups Basic Vegetable Stock (page 223)

2 tablespoons unsalted butter

1 large Spanish onion, chopped

3 garlic cloves, minced

4 poblano chilies, seeded and chopped

1 dried chipotle chile, minced

1 chipotle chile in adobo with ½
teaspoon sauce, minced*

1 tablespoon dried Mexican oregano
(see Ingredient Index, page 240), or
regular dried oregano

2 bay leaves

2 teaspoons kosher salt

6 medium Idaho potatoes, peeled, halved
lengthwise, and cut into 1-inch cubes

2 cups grated Queso Blanco* or
Monterey Jack cheese

½ cup crumbled feta cheese

½ cup heavy cream

½ cup chopped fresh cilantro

1. Combine the corn cobs and vegetable stock in a large stockpot over medium
   heat. Bring to a boil, reduce heat, partially cover, and simmer for 30 minutes.
   Remove the cobs with a slotted spoon and discard. Reserve 6 cups of the stock
   and set aside until ready to use.

2. Melt the butter in a large stockpot over medium heat. Add the onion, 2 of the
   garlic cloves, and poblano chilies and sweat for 4 minutes, until tender.

3. Add the dried chipotle, chipotle in adobo with sauce, oregano, bay leaves, and
   salt and stir to coat the vegetables.

4. Add the corn stock, corn, and potatoes and bring the mixture to a boil. Reduce
   the heat, partially cover, and simmer for 30 minutes.

5. Add the cheeses and heavy cream and simmer until the cheese melts.

*Available in Mexican specialty stores and gourmet markets.

6. Remove the bay leaves and puree about one quarter of the chowder in a blender or food processor until smooth.

7. Return the puree to the pot and mix well.

8. Remove the pot from the heat and stir in the remaining garlic clove and chopped cilantro.

9. To serve, ladle the soup into bowls and serve.

MAKES 12 CUPS.

CORN CHOWDER WITH CILANTRO

VARIATION:

CORN CHOWDER WITH
SHRIMP

Stir in 1 pound cooked,
peeled, and deveined
medium shrimp at step
4. Proceed with the
recipe as directed.

8 ears fresh corn, kernels sliced from
   cob and cobs reserved, about 4 cups
8 cups Basic Vegetable Stock (page
   223), or mineral water
3 garlic cloves, minced
1 chipotle chile in adobo with ½
   teaspoon sauce, minced*
2 tablespoons sugar

2½ teaspoons kosher salt
2 red bell peppers, halved, seeded, and
   cut into ¼-inch pieces
1 cup buttermilk
1 cup heavy cream
½ cup chopped fresh cilantro
1 tablespoon fresh lime juice
½ cup chopped scallions

1. Combine the corn cobs and stock in a large stockpot over medium heat. Bring to
   a boil, reduce heat, partially cover, and simmer for 30 minutes. Remove the cobs
   with a slotted spoon and discard. Reserve 2 cups of the stock and set aside until
   ready to use.

2. Blanch the corn kernels in rapidly boiling water for 4 minutes. Drain and transfer all but 2 cups of the corn to a blender or food processor.

3. Add the corn stock, garlic, chipotle in adobo with sauce, sugar, and salt and
   puree until smooth.

4. Transfer the mixture to a large bowl and stir in the remaining 2 cups of corn,
   red peppers, buttermilk, heavy cream, cilantro, and lime juice.

5. Refrigerate until ready to serve.

6. To serve, ladle the soup into bowls and top with the chopped scallions.

MAKES 10 CUPS.

*Available in Mexican specialty stores and gourmet markets.

POLENTA, RED BEANS, AND ITALIAN SAUSAGE

1   tablespoon olive oil

½   pound sweet Italian sausage (about 2 links), casing removed, crumbled

½   pound hot (spicy) Italian sausage (about 2 links), casing removed, crumbled

1   large Spanish onion, chopped

2   celery stalks, chopped

2   garlic cloves, minced

2   teaspoons dried thyme leaves

2   bay leaves

½   teaspoon ground black pepper

1   pound cranberry or Borlotti beans, rinsed and picked over to remove debris

10   cups Blonde Chicken Stock (page 226), or mineral water

1   (28-ounce) can whole tomatoes, drained and diced

½   cup instant polenta

1   bunch broccoli rabe, chopped

3   fresh sage leaves, minced

2½ teaspoons kosher salt

1. Heat the oil in a large stockpot over medium heat. Add the sausage and sauté 5 minutes, until golden brown. Remove the sausage with a slotted spoon, reserving the oil in the pan; set aside.

2. Add the onion, celery, and garlic to the pan and sweat for 4 minutes, until tender.

3. Add the thyme, bay leaves, and pepper and stir to coat the vegetables.

4. Add the beans, stock, and tomatoes and bring the mixture to a boil. Reduce the heat, partially cover, and simmer for 1 to 2 hours, until the beans are tender.

5. Stir in the sausage.

6. Gradually add the polenta in a thin stream, stirring constantly. Simmer for 5 minutes, stirring constantly, until the mixture is thick and smooth.

7. Remove from the heat, stir in the broccoli rabe, sage, and salt, cover, and let steep for 1 minute.

8. To serve, remove the bay leaves and ladle the soup into bowls.

MAKES 12 CUPS.

POSOLE

One day, a woman came into Daily Soup and had a bowl of our Posole. Three hours later, she returned with eight friends. She was from Mexico; she loved Posole, and she had trouble finding it in New York. Posole is a communal dish, and she obviously felt she couldn't eat alone. It was flattering to hear eight Posole lovers from Queens, New York discuss the authenticity of our soup.

1   3-pound boneless pork butt, trimmed
1   calf's foot,* cut up
6   cups Blonde Chicken Stock (page 226)
1   (28-ounce) can whole tomatoes, drained and diced
4   medium white onions, chopped
2   garlic cloves, minced
1   tablespoon dried Mexican oregano (see Ingredient Index, page 240), or regular dried oregano

1   chipotle pepper in adobo with ½ teaspoon sauce, minced**
2   teaspoons kosher salt
½   teaspoon ground black pepper
1   (15½-ounce) can hominy, drained
1   bunch kale, chopped
2   tablespoons fresh lime juice
½   cup chopped scallions

1. Preheat the oven to 325 degrees.
2. Combine the pork butt, calf's foot, and stock in a large stockpot over medium heat. Bring to a boil, reduce heat, and simmer for 30 minutes.
3. Skim the grease from the top, add the tomatoes, onions, garlic, oregano, chipotle in adobo with sauce, salt, and pepper. Bring to a boil, remove from the heat, cover, place in the oven, and braise for 2 hours.
4. Remove the pan from the oven, remove the pork butt and calf's foot with a slotted spoon, and when cool enough to handle, pull the skin from the calf's foot, discard the bones, slice the skin into thin strips, and return to the pot.

5. Cut the pork into bite-size pieces and return to the pot.

6. Place the pot over medium heat and add the hominy. Bring to a boil, reduce heat, and simmer for 20 minutes.

7. Stir in the kale and lime juice and simmer for 2 minutes to heat through.

8. To serve, ladle the soup into bowls and top with the chopped scallions.

MAKES 12 CUPS.

POTATO

JUST LIKE SWITZERLAND, potatoes are neutral. They have a subtle taste of their own, but they quickly absorb the flavor of stocks, vegetables, meats, and spices. Potatoes are to soup what cream cheese is to the bagel—a perfect marriage. We use them for their versatility, smooth texture, delicate flavor, and ideal cooking properties. Plus, everyone loves potatoes.

Potatoes can be pureed to make a velvety-smooth soup (creating a *mock cream*), or they can stand on their own, as big chunks in a hearty stew. Some people soak potatoes after cutting them to prevent browning from oxidation. Great—they're not brown, but they're not as starchy either (potatoes lose their starch content as they absorb water). The result is a watered down soup with diminished flavor. For best results, cut the potatoes and throw them right into the pot. If there's any browning, the soup will rinse it off.

Potato varieties, as wonderful as they all are, are not necessarily interchangeable. The potatoes you use for French fries (Russet) are not the same as those for mashing (Yukon Gold), and potato salad requires a different variety altogether. We use Chef potatoes (California White) or Yukon Gold because they hold their shape during long cooking times. Idaho Russet potatoes may also be used.

Sweet potatoes are a different story altogether. They're higher in sugar and lower in starch than the other spuds, and their sweet flavor dominates the soup. And, sweet potatoes break down much faster, completely dissolving when cooked too long—so be careful not to overcook them.

MEAT • SPICY

BOGOTA FOUR POTATO CHOWDER WITH CHICKEN

4 tablespoons peanut oil
1 whole chicken (about 4 pounds), cut up (see page 14)
8 cups mineral or filtered water
1 large Spanish onion, chopped
2 celery stalks, chopped
2 red bell peppers, seeded and chopped
3 garlic cloves, minced
1 habañero chile pepper, halved and seeded
2½ teaspoons ground cumin seeds
2 teaspoons kosher salt

1 teaspoon paprika
¼ teaspoon cayenne
4 purple potatoes, peeled and cut into 1-inch cubes
3 Yukon Gold potatoes, peeled and cut into 1-inch cubes
3 red bliss potatoes, cut into 1-inch cubes
1 Idaho potato, peeled and diced
½ cup heavy cream
½ cup chopped fresh cilantro

1. Heat 2 tablespoons of the oil in a large stockpot over medium heat. Add the chicken pieces and brown on all sides. Add the water, bring to a boil, reduce heat, and simmer for 10 minutes, until the chicken is cooked through. Remove the chicken with a slotted spoon, reserve the poaching liquid, and when cool enough to handle remove the meat from the bones and set aside. Strain the poaching liquid to remove solids, reserving 6 cups, and set aside.*

2. In a blender or food processor, puree the onion, celery, red peppers, 2 of the garlic cloves, and habañero chile.

3. Heat the remaining 2 tablespoons of oil in a large stockpot over medium heat and add the pureed onion mixture. Sweat for 4 minutes, until tender.

*To de-fat the stock, refrigerate for 1 hour, until a fat layer forms on the surface. Skim the layer of fat off the top and discard.

4. Add the cumin, salt, paprika, and cayenne and stir to coat the vegetables.
5. Return 4 cups of the chicken poaching liquid to the pot and add the chicken and all four potato varieties.
6. Bring to a boil, reduce heat, partially cover, and simmer for 20 minutes, adding remaining chicken stock if necessary.
7. Stir in the heavy cream.
8. Remove from the heat and stir in the remaining garlic clove and cilantro.
9. To serve, ladle the soup into bowls and serve.

MAKES 12 CUPS.

FRENCH GARLIC SAUSAGE AND POTATO

1	pound Safrom Saucisson a L'ail		8	medium Idaho potatoes, peeled, halved lengthwise, and cut into 1-inch cubes
6	cups mineral or filtered water		1	(28-ounce) can whole tomatoes, drained and diced
2	tablespoons unsalted butter		4	cups mineral or filtered water
1	large Spanish onion, chopped		½	cup heavy cream
2	celery stalks, chopped		3	tablespoons Dijon mustard
2	leeks, rinsed well and chopped		1	head escarole, chopped
2	teaspoons dried thyme leaves		1	teaspoon minced fresh garlic
2	bay leaves		¼	cup chopped fresh Italian parsley
2	teaspoons kosher salt			
½	teaspoon ground black pepper			

COOK'S NOTE:

Saucisson a L'ail (French for *garlic sausage*) is a smoke-cured pork sausage made with garlic, white wine and spices. You can also substitute Italian Cotechino (Ko-te-KEE-noh) sausage, which is made with similar ingredients.

1. Combine the sausage and water in a large stockpot over medium heat. Bring to a boil and poach the sausage for 15 minutes. Remove the sausage with a slotted spoon, reserving 2 cups of the poaching liquid. When cool enough to handle, slice the sausage crosswise into rounds, and then each round into quarters; set aside.

2. Melt the butter in the large stockpot over medium heat. Add the onion, celery, and leeks and sweat for 4 minutes, until tender.

3. Add the thyme, bay leaves, salt, and pepper and stir to coat the vegetables.

4. Return the sausage to the pan and add the reserved poaching liquid, potatoes, tomatoes, and water. Bring to a boil, reduce heat, partially cover, and simmer for 20 minutes, until the potatoes are tender.

5. Stir in the heavy cream and Dijon mustard.

6. Remove the bay leaves, puree about one quarter of the soup in a blender or food processor until smooth, and return to the pot.

7. Remove from the heat, stir in the escarole and garlic, cover, and let steep for 1 minute.

8. To serve, ladle the soup into bowls and top with the chopped parsley.

MAKES 12 CUPS.

NEW ENGLAND CLAM CHOWDER

VARIATION:

**NEW ENGLAND
LOBSTER CHOWDER**
First, place a live 2 to
3 pound lobster in a
large pot of rapidly
boiling water and cook
for 10 minutes. Drain
and reserve 6 cups of
the poaching liquid.
Remove the lobster
meat from the tail,
body, and claws and
cut into 1-inch cubes.
Pick up the recipe at
step 2 (sweat onion
and celery in butter).
Add the lobster broth
when instructed to add
clam broth and pota-
toes (step 4). Add lob-
ster meat with the
garlic (step 7). Pro-
ceed with the recipe
as directed.

2   dozen quahog clams, or 3 dozen little
    necks, shells tightly closed, scrubbed
2   cups mineral or filtered water
½   cup white wine
2   shallots, chopped
2   garlic cloves, minced
2   tablespoons unsalted butter
1   large Spanish onion, chopped
2   celery stalks, chopped

2   teaspoons dried thyme leaves
2   bay leaves
2   teaspoons kosher salt
½   teaspoon ground black pepper
6   medium Idaho potatoes, peeled, halved
    lengthwise, and cut into 1-inch cubes
½   cup heavy cream
½   cup chopped fresh Italian parsley
½   cup soda crackers

1. Combine the clams, water, wine, shallots, and 1 minced garlic clove in a large
   stockpot over medium heat. Bring to a boil, cover, and steam until the shells
   open, about 7 minutes. Remove the clams with a slotted spoon, reserve the
   broth, and discard any shells that have not opened. When cool enough to handle, chop the clams into ¼-inch pieces and set aside (discard shells). Strain the
   clam broth to remove solids, add enough water to equal 6 cups, and set aside.

2. Melt the butter in a large stockpot over medium heat. Add the onion and celery
   and sweat for 4 minutes, until tender.

3. Add the thyme, bay leaves, salt, and pepper and stir to coat the vegetables.

4. Add the reserved broth, clams, and potatoes. Bring to a boil, reduce heat, partially cover, and simmer for 45 minutes, until the potatoes are tender and broken down.

5. Stir in the heavy cream and simmer for 1 minute to heat through.

6. Remove the bay leaves, puree about half of the soup in a blender or food processor, and return to the pot.

7. Stir in the remaining garlic clove and mix well.

8. To serve, ladle the soup into bowls and top with the parsley and soda crackers.

MAKES 10 CUPS.

NEW ZEALAND SWEET POTATO CHOWDER

This is the perfect soup for nights when you want dinner in less than 45 minutes. This soup cooks so quickly, it's borderline fast food. You can make this soup faster than the time it would take to read the recipe in a New Zealand accent. For you New Zealanders, try reading the recipe with a New York accent.

2	tablespoons unsalted butter
1	large Spanish onion, chopped
1	tablespoon sugar
2	teaspoons dried thyme leaves
2	bay leaves
2	teaspoons kosher salt
½	teaspoon ground black pepper
6	cups Basic Vegetable Stock (page 223)
4	sweet potatoes, peeled, halved lengthwise, and cut into 1-inch cubes

3	yams, peeled, halved lengthwise, and cut into 1-inch cubes
2	ears fresh corn, kernels sliced from cob, about 1 cup
1	cup heavy cream
1	teaspoon minced fresh garlic
½	cup chopped fresh curly parsley

1. Melt the butter in a large stockpot over medium heat. Add the onion and sugar and caramelize for 10 minutes, until tender and golden.
2. Add the thyme, bay leaves, salt, and pepper and stir to coat the onion.
3. Add the stock, sweet potatoes, yams, and corn and bring the mixture to a boil. Reduce the heat, partially cover, and simmer for 20 minutes, until the potatoes are tender.
4. Stir in the heavy cream.
5. Remove the bay leaves and puree about one quarter of the chowder in a blender or food processor until smooth.
6. Return the puree to the pot and stir in the garlic.
7. To serve, ladle the chowder into bowls and top with the chopped parsley.

MAKES 12 CUPS.

SALMON POTATO CHOWDER

2 tablespoons unsalted butter

1 large Spanish onion, chopped

2 celery stalks, chopped

1 fresh fennel bulb, chopped

2 teaspoons dried thyme leaves

1 whole teaspoon fennel seeds

2 bay leaves

2 teaspoons kosher salt

6 red bliss potatoes, cut into 1-inch cubes

4 cups Basic Vegetable Stock (page 223)

1 cup tomato juice

2 (1-pound) salmon fillets, skinned and cut into 1-inch cubes

1½ cups heavy cream

2 tablespoons chopped fresh tarragon

½ cup chopped fresh Italian parsley

1. Melt the butter in a large stockpot over medium heat. Add the onion, celery, and fennel and sweat for 4 minutes, until tender.

2. Add the thyme, fennel seeds, bay leaves, and salt and stir to coat the vegetables.

3. Add the potatoes, stock, and tomato juice and bring the mixture to a boil. Reduce the heat, partially cover, and simmer for 20 minutes.

4. Add salmon and simmer 2 minutes.

5. Remove from the heat and add the heavy cream and fresh tarragon.

6. To serve, remove the bay leaves, ladle the soup into bowls, and top with the chopped parsley.

MAKES 12 CUPS.

VICHYSSOISE

2 tablespoons unsalted butter
2 leeks, rinsed well and chopped
2 teaspoons dried thyme leaves
2 bay leaves
2½ teaspoons kosher salt
½ teaspoon ground black pepper
¼ teaspoon ground nutmeg
6 medium Idaho potatoes, peeled, halved lengthwise, and cut into 1-inch cubes

10 cups Basic Vegetable Stock (page 223), or mineral water
4 red bliss potatoes, halved and thinly sliced
2½ cups heavy cream
1 garlic clove, minced
½ cup chopped scallions

1. Melt the butter in a large stockpot over medium heat. Add the leeks and sweat for 4 minutes, until tender.

2. Add the thyme, bay leaves, salt, pepper, and nutmeg and stir to coat the leeks.

3. Add the Idaho potatoes and stock and bring to a boil. Reduce heat, partially cover, and simmer for 20 minutes, until the potatoes are tender.

4. Meanwhile, in a separate pot, cook the red potatoes in rapidly boiling salt water for 10 minutes, until just tender. Rinse under cold water to prevent further cooking and set aside until ready to use.

5. Remove the bay leaves from the soup and stir in the heavy cream and garlic.

6. Puree the soup with a hand blender or a food processor (pulsing on and off) until smooth, about 3 to 5 minutes. (Using a blender or a food processor on continuous speed may make the potato mixture "gummy.")

7. Stir in the red potatoes.

8. Refrigerate until ready to serve.

9. To serve, ladle the soup into bowls and top with the chopped scallions.

MAKES 12 CUPS.

MUSIC RECOMMENDATIONS

SOUP	MUSIC
Cuban Black Bean	Ricky Ricardo—*Suava Lita*
Bahian Seafood Stew	David Byrne—*On the Road to Nowhere*
Chicken Matzoh Ball	*Baruch attaw adonoi*
Yankee Bean	*Over There*
Jambalaya	*Jambalaya, Crawfish Pie Ya Filé, Gumbo*
Jamaican Pumpkin	Screamin' Jay Hawkins—*I Put A Spell on You*
Bouillabaisse (or French Onion)	Edith Piaf—*La Vie en Rose*
Winter Borscht with Beef Short Ribs	Tchaikovsky—*Boris Godunov*
Moroccan Lamb Stew	Crosby, Stills & Nash—*Marrakesh Express*
Yucatan Chicken Lime	Any Menudo song
Pineapple Shrimp	B52s—*Strobelight*

BEAN

DRIED BEANS ARE known as the "flatulent meat" because they have a reputation for producing gas. Some reports claim that soaking beans overnight prevents flatulence. We've tried this method and the results are negligible. Soaking beans just reduces cooking time, but that's cheating.

When you soak dried beans in water, they soften as they absorb the liquid. You *want* beans to absorb liquid—but not water because water has no taste. To make a rich, deep soup, don't soak the beans, just rinse them to remove any dirt and debris and then soften them in a broth that's loaded with spices and vegetables. As beans cook, they absorb flavors and, over time, they begin to break down. The starch (similar to the starch in potatoes and grains) is released and the broth thickens. It's best to thicken soups naturally, with long cooking times. The trade-off—flatulence for flavor—is worth the price, and it makes for good conversation.

If you feel compelled to soak your beans, at least do it in vegetable or chicken stock.

The Mexican herb *Epazote* is used in chilies and Mexican soups. Epazote is a known "carminitive," meaning it reduces gas. We add it to bean soup and bring new meaning to the "perfectly balanced meal" because the soup both increases and reduces gas simultaneously.

There are dozens of dried bean varieties at the market. Several "heirlooms"—old varieties that were once spurned by commercial growers—have made a comeback. They look dramatically different—some black as night, some speckled with little red flecks, and still others with ornate patterns—but they are all related to the kidney, black, and great Northern beans from American bean fields. Be advised that all beans, even the same variety, are not created equal and cooking times can vary tremendously. Beans that have been sitting on the shelf for a while take longer to soften. The amount of stirring during the cooking process also affects the cooking time because there are different temperature pockets throughout the soup. Stirring the soup disperses these pockets and promotes even temperatures throughout the pot. It also prevents the beans at the bottom from burning.

LABORATORY TECHNICIAN'S NOTE:
Salt toughens beans if added too early in the cooking process, so add it at the end, just before serving.

BLACK BEAN WITH RICE AND GUACAMOLE

2	tablespoons peanut oil
1	large Spanish onion, chopped
2	celery stalks, chopped
1	habañero chile pepper, seeded and minced
1	teaspoon minced fresh garlic
2	teaspoons ground cumin seeds
2	teaspoons dried thyme leaves
2	bay leaves
1	pound black turtle beans, rinsed and picked over to remove debris
8	cups mineral or filtered water
1	(28-ounce) can whole tomatoes, drained and diced
½	teaspoon ground black pepper
¼	teaspoon cayenne
1	tablespoon sherry vinegar
1	teaspoon kosher salt

FOR THE RICE PILAF:

2	tablespoons peanut oil
1	cup white rice
1	teaspoon kosher salt
2	cups mineral or filtered water
2	scallions, chopped

FOR THE GUACAMOLE:

2	ripe Haas avocados,* peeled, pitted, and chopped
2	plum tomatoes, seeded and diced
1	small white onion, minced
1	serrano chile, seeded and minced
2	tablespoons chopped fresh cilantro
½	teaspoon kosher salt
¼	teaspoon ground black pepper

1. To make the soup, heat the oil in a large stockpot over medium heat. Add half of the onion and all of the celery, habañero, and garlic and sweat for 4 minutes, until tender.

2. Add the cumin, thyme, and bay leaves and stir to coat the vegetables.

*We like to use Haas avocados, the purplish-black variety from California. Because Haas avocados contain twice as much fat as the smaller, smooth-skin, green avocados from Florida, they have a rich and buttery flesh that is perfectly suited for our soups.

VARIATION:

BLACK BEAN WITH SWEET ITALIAN SAUSAGE—
In a large stockpot, sauté 1 pound of crumbled sweet Italian sausage in 2 tablespoons of oil until cooked through. Remove the sausage with a slotted spoon, reserving the oil in pan. Use the oil to sweat the onion, celery, habañero, and garlic (step 1). Proceed with the recipe as directed, except for the addition of rice and guacamole. After pureeing one quarter of the soup in a blender (step 4), add the cooked sausage and simmer for 2 minutes to heat through. Stir in the sherry and minced garlic (step 5) and serve.

3. Stir in the black beans, 6 cups of the water, tomatoes, pepper, and cayenne. Bring to a boil, reduce heat, partially cover, and simmer for 1 to 2 hours, until the beans are tender.

4. Puree about one quarter of the soup in a blender or food processor and return to the pot.

5. Remove from the heat and stir in the sherry, garlic, and salt.

6. Meanwhile, to make the rice, heat the oil in a medium saucepan over medium heat. Add the remaining onion and sauté for 2 minutes.

7. Stir in the rice and sauté for 2 minutes, until the rice is translucent.

8. Add the remaining 2 cups of water and salt, bring to a boil, reduce heat, cover, and simmer for 20 minutes, until the liquid is absorbed.

9. Add the scallions and toss with a fork.

10. To make the guacamole, combine all the ingredients in a medium bowl. Mix well with a fork to combine.

11. To serve, remove the bay leaves from the soup, spoon the rice mixture into the bottom of shallow soup bowls, ladle the soup over the top, and garnish with a spoonful of guacamole.

MAKES: 10 CUPS BLACK BEAN SOUP; 3 CUPS RICE MIXTURE; 1 1/2 CUPS GUACAMOLE.

CUBAN BLACK BEAN

2	tablespoons peanut oil
1	large Spanish onion, chopped
2	celery stalks, chopped
2	carrots, peeled and chopped
1	habañero chile pepper, seeded and diced
1	tablespoon ground cumin seeds
2	teaspoons dried thyme leaves
2	bay leaves
½	teaspoon ground black pepper
1	pound black turtle beans, rinsed and picked over to remove debris
1	(28-ounce) can whole tomatoes, drained and diced
6	cups mineral or filtered water
1	cup chopped scallions
1	tablespoon sherry vinegar
1	teaspoon minced fresh garlic
½	teaspoon habañero sauce, or other hot pepper sauce
1½	teaspoons kosher salt

1. Preheat the oven to 325 degrees.

2. Heat the oil in a large stockpot over medium heat. Add the onion, celery, carrots, and habañero pepper and sweat for 4 minutes, until tender.

3. Add the cumin, thyme, bay leaves, and pepper and stir to coat the vegetables.

4. Add the beans, tomatoes, and water and bring to a boil.

5. Remove from the heat, cover, and place in the oven to slow cook for 2 hours, until the beans are tender.

6. Remove from the oven and place the pot over low heat.

7. Remove the bay leaves, puree about one quarter of the soup in a blender or food processor, and return to the pot.

8. Remove from the heat and stir in ½ cup of the scallions, vinegar, garlic, hot sauce, and salt.

9. To serve, ladle the soup into bowls and top with the remaining scallions.

MAKES 12 CUPS.

VARIATION:

CUBAN BLACK BEAN WITH SHRIMP
After pureeing one quarter of the soup in a blender (step 7), stir in 1 pound of peeled and deveined medium shrimp and cook for 3 minutes, until the shrimp are bright red and cooked through. Remove from the heat and stir in the scallions, vinegar, garlic, hot sauce, and salt (step 8). Serve as directed.

MARRIAGE COUNSELOR'S NOTE:
The secret to the success of this soup is the two hours of braising in the oven. The ingredients have a chance to fully evolve and marry—making the soup well worth the wait.

GALICIAN WHITE BEAN
WITH CHORIZO

1	pound chorizo	½	teaspoon ground black pepper
6	cups mineral or filtered water	1	pound Great Northern beans, rinsed and picked over to remove debris
1	tablespoon olive oil		
¼	pound slab or presliced bacon, cut into ¼-inch cubes	2	medium potatoes, peeled, halved lengthwise, and cut into 1-inch cubes
1	large Spanish onion, chopped	6	cups Basic Vegetable Stock (page 223), or mineral water
3	carrots, peeled and chopped		
3	garlic cloves, minced	1	bunch radish leaves, chopped
2	teaspoons dried thyme leaves	¼	cup dry vermouth
1	teaspoon paprika	2	teaspoons kosher salt
2	bay leaves	½	cup chopped scallions

1. Combine the chorizo and water in a large stockpot over medium heat. Bring to a boil, reduce heat, and poach for 10 minutes. Remove the chorizo with a slotted spoon, reserving 2 cups of the poaching liquid. When cool enough to handle, slice the chorizo into rounds and set aside.

2. Heat the oil in a large stockpot over medium heat. Add the bacon and sauté for 10 minutes, until golden brown and the fat is rendered.

3. Add the onion, carrots, and 2 of the garlic cloves and sweat for 4 minutes, until tender.

4. Add the thyme, paprika, bay leaves, and pepper and stir to coat the vegetables.

5. Add the reserved poaching liquid, beans, potatoes, and stock and bring the mixture to a boil. Reduce the heat, partially cover, and simmer for 1 to 2 hours, until the beans are tender.

6. Stir in the sliced chorizo and simmer for 2 minutes.

7. Remove from the heat and stir in the radish leaves, vermouth, and salt and remaining garlic clove.

8. To serve, remove the bay leaves, ladle the soup into bowls, and top with the chopped scallions.

MAKES 12 CUPS.

TUSCAN MULTI-BEAN

2 tablespoons olive oil

1 large Spanish onion, chopped

2 celery stalks, chopped

3 garlic cloves, minced

2 teaspoons dried rosemary

2 bay leaves

½ teaspoon ground black pepper

½ cup black turtle beans, rinsed and picked over to remove debris

½ cup Great Northern beans, rinsed and picked over to remove debris

½ cup cranberry or Borlotti beans, rinsed and picked over to remove debris

½ cup dried chickpeas (garbanzo beans), rinsed and drained

½ cup French lentils, rinsed and picked over to remove debris

8 cups Basic Vegetable Stock (page 223), or mineral water

1 (28-ounce) can whole tomatoes, drained and diced

½ cup uncooked white rice

1 cup shelled fava beans or frozen lima beans, thawed

2 teaspoons kosher salt

½ cup chopped scallions

HOUSE-KEEPER'S NOTE:
This is a great end of the month soup, when it's time to clean out the pantry. Add a little bit of everything to get great results.

1. Heat the oil in a large stockpot over medium heat. Add the onion, celery, and 2 cloves of the garlic and sweat for 4 minutes, until tender.

2. Add the rosemary, bay leaves, and pepper and stir to coat the vegetables.

3. Add the beans, lentils, stock, and tomatoes and bring the mixture to a boil. Reduce the heat, partially cover, and simmer for 1 to 2 hours, until the beans are tender.

4. Stir in the rice and simmer for 20 minutes.

5. Stir in the fava beans and simmer for 2 minutes.

6. Remove from the heat and stir in the salt and remaining garlic clove.

7. To serve, remove the bay leaves, ladle the soup into bowls, and garnish with the chopped scallions.

MAKES 10 CUPS.

TUSCAN SHRIMP AND WHITE BEAN

2 tablespoons olive oil

4 leeks, rinsed well and chopped

2 celery stalks, chopped

3 garlic cloves, minced

1 bunch fresh thyme, leaves chopped and stems reserved

2 teaspoons dried rosemary

2 bay leaves

½ teaspoon ground black pepper

1 pound cannellini (white kidney) beans, rinsed and picked over to remove debris

8 cups Basic Vegetable Stock (page 223) or mineral water

1 (28-ounce) can whole tomatoes, drained and diced

1 pound medium shrimp, peeled and deveined

1 tablespoon balsamic vinegar

2 teaspoons kosher salt

1. Heat the oil in a large stockpot over medium heat. Add the leeks, celery, and 2 of the garlic cloves and sweat for 4 minutes, until tender.

2. Tie the thyme stems together with string and add to the pot with the rosemary, bay leaves, and pepper. Stir to coat the vegetables.

3. Add the beans, stock, and tomatoes and bring the mixture to a boil. Reduce the heat, partially cover, and simmer for 1 hour, until the beans are tender.

4. Add the shrimp and simmer for 3 minutes, until the shrimp are bright red and cooked through.

5. Remove from the heat and stir in the remaining garlic clove, chopped thyme, balsamic vinegar, and salt.

6. To serve, remove the thyme stems and bay leaves and ladle the soup into bowls.

MAKES 12 CUPS.

ZUPPA DI FAGIOLI

2 tablespoons olive oil

1 large Spanish onion, chopped

2 celery stalks, chopped

1 bulb fresh fennel (about ½ pound), chopped into 1-inch pieces

3 garlic cloves, minced

2 teaspoons dried thyme leaves

2 bay leaves

½ teaspoon ground black pepper

1 pound cranberry or Borlotti beans, rinsed and picked over to remove debris

6 cups Basic Vegetable Stock (page 223) or mineral water

1 (28-ounce) can whole tomatoes, drained and diced

1 (3-inch) piece Parmesan cheese rind

1 bunch mustard greens, chopped

3 fresh sage leaves, minced

2 teaspoons kosher salt

VARIATION:

PASTA E FAGIOLI

Stir in elbow, ditalini, or other small-shaped pasta after step 3. Simmer until the pasta is tender and serve as directed.

1. Heat the oil in a large stockpot over medium heat. Add the onion, celery, fennel, and 2 of the garlic cloves and sweat for 4 minutes, until tender.

2. Add the thyme, bay leaves, and pepper and stir to coat the vegetables.

3. Add the beans, stock, tomatoes, and Parmesan rind and bring the mixture to a boil. Reduce the heat, partially cover, and simmer for 2 hours, until the beans are tender.

4. Remove from the heat and stir in the mustard greens, sage, salt, and remaining garlic clove. Cover and let steep for 1 minute.

5. To serve, remove the bay leaves and Parmesan rind and ladle the soup into bowls.

MAKES 10 CUPS.

WILD MUSHROOM, CRANBERRY BEAN, AND KALE

4 tablespoons olive oil	3 garlic cloves, minced
1 pound button or cremini mushrooms, stems removed and reserved, caps sliced	10 fresh thyme stems, leaves chopped and stems reserved
½ pound oyster mushrooms, stems removed and reserved, caps sliced	2 teaspoons dried rosemary
	2 bay leaves
	½ teaspoon ground black pepper
½ pound shiitake or porcini mushrooms, stems removed and reserved, caps sliced	½ pound cranberry or Borlotti beans, rinsed and picked over to remove debris
8 cups mineral or filtered water	1 (28-ounce) can whole tomatoes, drained and diced
½ cup white port or white wine	1 bunch kale, chopped
1 large Spanish onion, chopped	1 tablespoon balsamic vinegar
2 celery stalks, chopped	2 teaspoons kosher salt
2 leeks, rinsed well and chopped	

1. Heat 2 tablespoons of the oil in a large stockpot over medium heat. Add the mushroom stems and a few button mushroom caps and sweat for 5 minutes, until tender and releasing juice. Add the water and white port and bring the mixture to a boil. Reduce the heat, partially cover, and simmer for 20 minutes. Strain the stock through a fine sieve to remove solids, reserving 5 cups of the liquid; set aside.

2. Heat the remaining 2 tablespoons of the oil in a large stockpot over medium heat. Add the onion, celery, leeks, and 2 cloves of the garlic and sweat for 4 minutes, until tender.

3. Tie the thyme stems together with string and add to the pot with the rosemary, bay leaves, and pepper. Stir to coat the vegetables.

4. Add the mushrooms and sauté 5 minutes.

5. Add the reserved mushroom liquid, beans, and tomatoes. Bring the mixture to a boil, reduce heat, partially cover, and simmer for 2 hours, until the beans are tender.

6. Remove from the heat and stir in the kale, balsamic vinegar, chopped thyme, salt, and remaining garlic clove. Cover and let steep 1 minute.

7. To serve, remove the thyme stems and bay leaves and ladle the soup into bowls.

MAKES 12 CUPS.

YANKEE BEAN WITH HAM

We served Yankee Bean on opening day at our first store. We didn't sell very much at all. The next time Leslie put it on the menu, we all voted that we should never serve that soup again. It wasn't as popular as other soups. A few months later, Leslie snuck it onto the menu and of course it sold out by 2:00 P.M. This taught us that one test is not always enough.

2 tablespoons canola oil	1 smoked ham hock (about ½ pound)
1 large Spanish onion, chopped	4 medium Idaho potatoes, peeled, halved
2 celery stalks, chopped	lengthwise, and cut into 1-inch cubes
2 teaspoons dried thyme leaves	½ pound smoked ham, bought unsliced
2 bay leaves	and cut into ¼-inch cubes
½ teaspoon ground black pepper	1 tablespoon balsamic vinegar
8 cups mineral or filtered water	1 teaspoon minced fresh garlic
1 pound Great Northern beans, rinsed	1 teaspoon kosher salt
and picked over to remove debris	½ cup chopped scallions

1. Heat the oil in a large stockpot over medium heat. Add the onion and celery and sweat for 4 minutes, until tender.

2. Add the thyme, bay leaves, and pepper and stir to coat the vegetables.

3. Add the water, beans, ham hock, and potatoes, bring to a boil, reduce heat, partially cover, and simmer for 2 hours, until the beans are tender and the potatoes are broken down.

4. Remove the ham hock and bay leaves and stir in the cubed ham, balsamic vinegar, garlic, and salt. Simmer for 2 minutes to heat through.

5. To serve, ladle the soup into bowls and top with the chopped scallions.

MAKES 12 CUPS.

Dear Soup Guys,

Just yesterday I ordered one of your delicious soups and saw the adorable black and white poster of the dog licking his mouth after eating a bowl of your soup. I was actually wondering how I could get a poster like that for myself. I would love to have my Daily Soup, in my own home, while staring at the Daily Soup Dog.

Dear Daily Soup People,

We have not been receiving our daily E-mail menu. We miss it. We are loyal customers, some would even call us fanatics. We love your choices. We love your Blue-Pots. We love how you let us know what's vegetarian, what's spicy, and what's low fat. It's like you're concerned about us, and to prove it, you give us cookies and fruit with our order. Several of us here get the soup list, and several more depend on us to print it out for them. But all week, we have received nothing. Have you deleted us? Have you quit on us? Have we angered you by complaining about the Chilled Thai Melon (it was just one of us, and we can have that person fired, if it will bring back our daily soup list . . .)? Let's make up. We're willing to see a therapist to work things out. Just send us our Daily Soup list. Thanks.

CHILI

PATIENCE IS CRUCIAL when making chili. Rushing the process produces a shallow or immature chili, and no one wants to spend time with an immature chili. It's fascinating to taste and smell chili at each stage of its growth. You'll enjoy watching your chili go from an immature adolescent to a sophisticated adult. Take pictures. The time goes fast.

In a bad or immature chili, you can detect the raw taste of cumin and chili powder. In a properly made adult chili, the spices create a smooth finish. Chili spice mixtures should balance aroma, heat, sweetness, and tanginess.

Oil is used in chili to carry the spices throughout the soup. Much like Robin Hood, oil steals flavor from the rich spices and gives it to the meat. And nobody gets hurt. First, vegetables are caramelized in oil to create a base flavor. Then, spices are added to give a bonus flavor to the oil, the raw taste is cooked off, and the inherent flavor of each spice comes alive. Next, the meat is added and browned, and a crazy fusion take place as the ingredients start to influence each other. As the meat cooks, it trades its fat for the seasoned oil.

Next, tomatoes are added to impart acidity. If you sample the chili at this point, it will taste raw. Over time, the tomatoes *spread out* and lend their distinct flavor. Once this happens, you can add the beans and stock. The whole mixture should then cook for one to two hours, to give the beans a chance to soften and soak up all the *love* you put in.

CHICKEN BLACK BEAN CHILI

**TURKEY
RED BEAN CHILI**
Substitute red kidney beans for black. Sauté 1 pound of ground turkey meat in 2 tablespoons oil until browned and cooked through, about 5 to 7 minutes. Remove the meat with a slotted spoon, reserving the oil in the pan. Pick up the recipe where instructed to sweat the vegetables in oil (step 3). Add the turkey meat when instructed to add chicken, 8 cups vegetable stock or water and tomatoes (step 5). Proceed with the recipe as directed.

1 pound black turtle beans, rinsed and picked over to remove debris
16 cups mineral or filtered water
4 tablespoons peanut oil
1 whole chicken (about 4 pounds), cut up (see page 14)
3 medium white onions, chopped
2 carrots, peeled and chopped
2 red bell peppers, seeded and chopped
2 Pickled Jalapeños (page 237), diced
1 habañero chile pepper, seeded and chopped
2 tablespoons chili powder
2 teaspoons ground cumin seeds
1½ teaspoons ground coriander seeds
2 bay leaves
1 tablespoon dried Mexican oregano (see Ingredient Index, page 240), or regular dried oregano
2 teaspoons kosher salt
1 (28-ounce) can whole tomatoes, diced
½ cup uncooked bulgur wheat
1 teaspoon habañero pepper sauce
1 teaspoon minced fresh garlic
½ cup chopped fresh cilantro

1. Place the beans in a large stockpot. Pour over 8 cups of the water, bring to a boil, reduce heat, partially cover, and simmer for 1 hour, until the beans are tender. Set aside until ready to use.

2. Meanwhile, heat 2 tablespoons of oil in a large stockpot over medium heat. Add the chicken pieces and brown on all sides. Add the remaining water, bring to a boil, reduce heat, and simmer for 10 minutes, until the chicken is cooked through. Remove the chicken with a slotted spoon, reserve the poaching liquid, and when cool enough to handle remove the meat from the bones and set aside. Strain the poaching liquid to remove solids, reserving 6 cups, and set aside.*

3. Heat the remaining 2 tablespoons of oil in the pot and add the onions, carrots, bell peppers, jalapeños, and habañero pepper. Sweat for 4 minutes, until tender.

*To de-fat the stock, refrigerate for 1 hour, until a fat layer forms on the surface. Skim the layer of fat off the top and discard.

4. Add the chili powder, cumin, coriander, bay leaves, oregano, and salt and stir to coat vegetables. Simmer 5 minutes to cook the spices and increase flavor.

5. Return the chicken to the pot and add the reserved poaching liquid and tomatoes. Bring to a boil, reduce heat, partially cover, and simmer for 20 minutes.

6. Return the beans to the pan and stir in the bulgur. Simmer for 20 minutes, until the bulgur is tender.

7. Remove from heat and stir in the habañero sauce and garlic.

8. To serve, remove the bay leaves, ladle the chili into bowls, and top with the chopped cilantro.

MAKES 12 CUPS.

VARIATION:

**VENISON
WHITE BEAN CHILI**
Substitute white cannellini beans for black. Sauté 1 pound of cubed stewing venison in 2 tablespoons of oil until browned and cooked through, about 5 to 7 minutes. Remove the meat with a slotted spoon, reserving the oil in the pan. Pick up the recipe where instructed to sweat the vegetables in oil (step 3). Add the venison when instructed to add the chicken, 8 cups vegetable stock or water and tomatoes (step 5). Proceed with the recipe as directed.

BRAISED PORK CHILI WITH BLACK BEANS AND CORN

1	pound black turtle beans, rinsed and picked over to remove debris
8	cups mineral or filtered water
1	(3-pound) boneless pork butt, trimmed and cut into 1-inch cubes
6	cups Blonde Chicken Stock (page 226), or mineral water
1	(28-ounce) can whole tomatoes, diced
3	medium white onions, chopped
2	celery stalks, chopped
2	green bell peppers, seeded and chopped
2	garlic cloves, minced
1	habañero chile pepper, seeded and minced
2	Pickled Jalapeños (page 237), minced
3	tablespoons chili powder
1	tablespoon dried Mexican oregano (see Ingredient Index, page 240) or regular dried oregano
2	teaspoons kosher salt
½	teaspoon ground black pepper
¼	cup bulgur wheat
2	cups fresh cob corn
½	cup chopped scallions

1. Place the beans in a large stockpot. Cover with the water and bring to a boil. Reduce heat, partially cover, and simmer for 1 hour.

2. Preheat the oven to 325 degrees.

3. Combine the pork cubes and stock in a second large stockpot over medium heat. Bring to a boil, reduce heat, and simmer for 30 minutes.

4. Skim the grease from the top, add the beans, tomatoes, onions, celery, green peppers, garlic, habañero, jalapeños, chili powder, oregano, salt, and pepper. Bring to a boil, remove from heat, cover, place in the oven to braise for 1 hour. Remove the pot from the oven and place over medium heat.

5. Add the bulgur and simmer for 20 minutes.

6. Stir in the corn and simmer for 2 minutes.

7. To serve, ladle the chili into bowls and top with chopped scallions.

MAKES 12 CUPS.

CHILI CON CARNE

½ pound black turtle beans, rinsed and picked over to remove debris

½ pound red kidney beans, rinsed and picked over to remove debris

10 cups mineral or filtered water

2 tablespoons peanut oil

1 pound ground beef

½ pound sweet Italian sausage (about 2 links), casing removed and crumbled

½ pound hot Italian sausage (about 2 links), casing removed and crumbled

1 large Spanish onion, chopped

2 celery stalks, chopped

2 green bell peppers, seeded and chopped

3 garlic cloves, minced

2 Pickled Jalapeños (page 237), minced

2 tablespoons chili powder

1 tablespoon dried Mexican oregano (see Ingredient Index, page 240), or regular dried oregano

2 teaspoons ground cumin seeds

1½ teaspoons ground coriander seeds

2 bay leaves

2 teaspoons kosher salt

1 (28-ounce) can whole tomatoes, diced

1 to 2 teaspoons habañero sauce

½ cup chopped scallions

½ cup sour cream

1. Place the black and red beans in a large stockpot, pour over enough mineral water to cover, and place over medium high heat. Bring to a boil, reduce heat, partially cover, and simmer for 1 to 2 hours, until the beans are tender. Drain, reserving 2 cups liquid, and set aside until ready to use.

2. Meanwhile, heat the oil in a large stockpot over medium heat. Add the beef and sausages and sauté for 5 minutes, until browned. Remove the meat with a slotted spoon, reserving the oil in the pan, and set aside.

3. Add the onion, celery, bell peppers, 2 of the garlic cloves, and jalapeños to the oil and sweat for 4 minutes, until tender.

4. Add the chili powder, oregano, cumin, coriander, bay leaves, and salt and stir to coat the vegetables. Cook for 5 minutes, until the spices are fragrant.

5. Add the tomatoes and simmer for 2 minutes.

6. Return the meat to the pan and add the beans and the 2 cups of bean cooking liquid. Bring to a boil, reduce heat, partially cover, and simmer for 20 minutes.

7. Remove from heat and stir in the remaining garlic clove and habañero sauce.

8. To serve, remove the bay leaves, ladle the chili into bowls, and top with the chopped scallions and sour cream.

MAKES 12 CUPS.

CINCINNATI CHILI

1 pound red kidney beans, rinsed and
  picked over to remove debris

8 cups mineral or filtered water

2 tablespoons peanut oil

1 pound ground beef

1 large Spanish onion, chopped

2 garlic cloves, minced

2 tablespoons chili powder

1 tablespoon dried oregano

1½ teaspoons ground coriander seeds

¼ teaspoon ground cinnamon

¼ teaspoon ground allspice

¼ teaspoon ground cloves

¼ teaspoon cayenne

2 bay leaves

2 teaspoons kosher salt

1 (28-ounce) can whole tomatoes, diced

3 cups cooked spaghetti

1 cup grated cheddar cheese

1. Place the beans in a large stockpot. Pour over enough mineral water to cover and place over medium high heat. Bring to a boil, reduce heat, partially cover, and simmer for 1 to 2 hours, until the beans are tender. Drain, reserving 1 cup of the cooking liquid, and set aside until ready to use.

2. Meanwhile, heat the oil in a large stockpot over medium heat. Add the beef and cook for 5 minutes, until browned. Remove the beef from the pot with a slotted spoon, reserving the oil in pan; set aside.

3. Add the onion and garlic to the oil and sweat for 4 minutes, until tender.

4. Add the chili powder, oregano, coriander, cinnamon, allspice, cloves, cayenne, bay leaves, and salt and stir to coat. Cook for 5 minutes, until the spices are fragrant.

5. Add the tomatoes and simmer for 2 minutes.

6. Return the beef to the pot and bring to a boil. Reduce heat, partially cover, and simmer for 10 minutes.

7. Stir in the beans with the bean cooking liquid and simmer for 10 minutes.

8. To serve, remove the bay leaves, ladle the chili over the spaghetti, and top with the grated cheddar.

MAKES 12 CUPS.

SOUTHWESTERN GREEN CHILI WITH CHICKEN

INTERFAITH COUNSELOR'S NOTE:
A fusion of Indian and Mexican cuisines, this soup is called "green" not because it looks green in color, but because of the abundance of green pepper varieties.

4	tablespoons peanut oil
1	whole chicken (about 4 pounds), cut up (see page 14)
8	cups mineral or filtered water
1	large Spanish onion, chopped
2	celery stalks, chopped
2	green bell peppers, seeded and chopped
2	poblano chile peppers, seeded and chopped
2	Pickled Jalapeño peppers (page 237), diced
2	tablespoons chili powder

2	teaspoons ground cumin seeds
2	teaspoons ground coriander seeds
2	bay leaves
2	teaspoons dried Mexican oregano (see Ingredient Index, page 240), or regular dried oregano
2	teaspoons kosher salt
1	(28-ounce) can whole tomatoes, diced
½	cup uncooked quinoa
2	cups frozen lima beans, thawed
1	teaspoon minced fresh garlic
½	cup chopped fresh cilantro

1. Heat 2 tablespoons of the oil in a large stockpot over medium heat. Add the chicken pieces and brown on all sides. Add the water, bring to a boil, reduce heat, and simmer for 10 minutes, until the chicken is cooked through. Remove the chicken with a slotted spoon, reserve the poaching liquid, and when cool enough to handle remove the meat from the bones and set aside. Strain the poaching liquid to remove solids, reserving 6 cups, and set aside.*

2. Heat the remaining 2 tablespoons of oil in the pot and add the onion, celery, bell peppers, poblano chile peppers, and jalapeños. Sweat for 4 minutes, until tender.

*To de-fat the stock, refrigerate for 1 hour, until a fat layer forms on the surface. Skim the layer of fat off the top and discard.

3. Add the chili powder, cumin, coriander, bay leaves, oregano, and salt and stir to coat the vegetables. Cook for 5 minutes, until the spices are fragrant.

4. Return the chicken to the pot and add the reserved poaching liquid and tomatoes. Bring to a boil, reduce heat, partially cover, and simmer for 20 minutes.

5. Add the quinoa and simmer for 10 minutes, until tender.

6. Stir in the lima beans and simmer for 2 minutes.

7. Remove from the heat and stir in the garlic.

8. To serve, remove the bay leaves, ladle the chili into bowls, and top with the chopped cilantro.

MAKES 12 CUPS.

FOUR-BEAN VEGETARIAN CHILI

¼ pound black turtle beans, rinsed and picked over to remove debris

¼ pound white kidney beans, rinsed and picked over to remove debris

¼ pound red kidney beans, rinsed and picked over to remove debris

8 cups mineral or filtered water

2 tablespoons peanut oil

1 large Spanish onion, chopped

2 celery stalks, chopped

2 green bell peppers, seeded and chopped

2 garlic cloves, minced

2 Pickled Jalapeños (page 237), minced

2 tablespoons chili powder

1 tablespoon dried Mexican oregano (see Ingredient Index, page 240), or regular dried oregano

2 teaspoons ground cumin seeds

1½ teaspoons ground coriander seeds

2 bay leaves

2 teaspoons kosher salt

1 (28-ounce) can whole tomatoes, diced

¼ cup bulgur wheat

2 cups frozen lima beans, thawed

1 to 2 teaspoons habañero or other hot sauce

3 cups cooked rice

½ cup chopped scallions

1. Place the beans in a large stockpot and pour over enough mineral water to cover. Bring to a boil, reduce heat, partially cover, and simmer for 1 to 2 hours, until the beans are tender. Drain, reserving 2 cups of the liquid, and set aside until ready to use.

2. Meanwhile, heat the oil in a large stockpot over medium heat. Add the onion, celery, bell peppers, garlic, and jalapeños and sweat for 4 minutes, until tender.

3. Add the chili powder, oregano, cumin, coriander, bay leaves, and salt and stir to coat the vegetables. Cook for 5 minutes, until the spices are fragrant.

4. Add the tomatoes and simmer for 2 minutes.

5. Add the beans, bean cooking liquid (from the white or red beans; black beans create a dark, murky liquid) and bulgur, bring to a boil, reduce heat, partially cover, and simmer for 20 minutes.

6. Add the lima beans and habañero sauce and simmer for 2 minutes.

7. To serve, remove the bay leaves, ladle the chili over rice, and top with the chopped scallions.

MAKES 12 CUPS.

MOVIES TO RENT WHILE YOU EAT SOUP

SOUP	MOVIE
Turkey Pot Pie	*Avalon*
Tomato Basil, Tomato Fennel,	*Attack of the Killer Tomatoes!*
Gazpacho	*Women on the Verge of a Nervous Breakdown*
Indian Black Lentil	*Yentl*
Indian Yellow Split Pea	*Mississippi Masala*
Lobster Mango with Avocado (cold)	*The Birdcage*
Cheddar Cheese with Potatoes and Bacon	*On the Waterfront*
Cream of Lentil	*Eraserhead*
Wild Mushroom Barley	*Alice in Wonderland*
New England Clam Chowder	*Hotel New Hampshire*
Borscht (cold)	*Reds*

Green Gumbo with Oysters	*The Exorcist*
Peking Duck	*Big Trouble in Little China*
Crawfish Étouffée	*Blaze*
Chicken and Seafood Jambalaya	*The Big Easy*
Tomato Maryland Crab	*Tin Men*
Braised Pork Chili with Black Beans and Corn	*Babe*
Bogota Four Potato Chowder with Chicken	*Missing*
Zuppa di Fagioli	*The Godfather: Part I*
Tuscan Multi-Bean	*Blazing Saddles*
Vichyssoise (cold)	*The French Lieutenant's Woman*

LENTIL AND PEA

IN TERMS OF cooking characteristics, lentils are similar to dried beans and peas. In the United States, we usually use French lentils, but there are dozens of varieties that are available but still unexplored in this country. In India, there are over sixty varieties and each has a different color, taste, texture, and cooking time.

All lentils are handpicked and sometimes pebbles are mixed in "accidentally" (actually, most of the time, as pebbles are intentionally added to increase the weight and get a higher price from lentil brokers). We have a whole department at Daily Soup dedicated to the cleaning and picking through of lentils. If pebbles were edible, we could easily make a hearty Curried Pebble Bisque.

All Indian lentils are cooked with curry and masala. Curry is a sauce and masala is a spice mixture. Technically, salt and pepper could be considered a masala. Once cooked with meat or vegetables, they would be considered part of a curry.

Most Indian masalas are a blend of twenty to thirty different spices, each boasting a different element—hot, sour, nutty, bitter, and salty. Individually, each spice would be overpowering or one-dimensional. But somehow, when you mix together cinnamon, cloves, cumin, cardamom, and turmeric, you get a subtle, delicate balance, almost like one complete spice.

Curries serve two purposes—they excite the tongue, and they're good for the body. Curries often make you sweat, helping you rid your body of toxins. Some spices are known for their antiseptic value, while some reduce flatulence, and others are touted for their aphrodisiac qualities. Actually, you could make a case that by *reducing flatulence*, certain spices automatically qualify as *aphrodisiacs*.

Split peas are the most prestigious of all dried peas. The word "split" is used almost exclusively to describe split pea soup. What makes split peas so desirable is their ability to break down to create a thick, creamy soup. Since whole peas don't break down, you get a more brothy soup when you cook with them. But don't worry about the whole pea, it has its place in Pea Parmesan (page 140) and pasta sauce, and it gets to keep a princess awake in fables.

Split pea is the mother of all soups, and recipes typically start with making a smoky stock using whole ham hocks. We eliminated ham hocks because split pea soup makes such a natural vegetarian meal. Recently, we've been dry-smoking our peas in applewood to get that same smoky flavor without adding meat.

We also cook our split pea soup with white wine for added depth. Alcohol is an acid, and it is an important ingredient in several of our soups. When you add wine, cognac, lemon juice, or vinegar early in the cooking process, the strong, tangy taste is diminished and the alcohol content is simmered off.

Although subtle, the flavor that remains is distinct and full-bodied. Sometimes a soup is *finished* (or completed) by adding wine or vinegar at the end. This technique adds a fresh, sharp quality to the soup.

Pea and other dense soups take a long time to cool. See the Temperature section in the beginning of the book for safely cooling these types of soups.

VEGETARIAN
CREAM OF LENTIL

LESLIE'S SECRET:

Seven cloves of garlic?? Yes. While the lentils cook, a thick garlic cream simmers and reduces. The sweetness of both the cream and the garlic meld together as they cook, and this flavor adds incredible depth to the soup (one secret we hate to give away . . .).

2	tablespoons unsalted butter	1	pound French lentils, rinsed and picked over to remove debris
1	large Spanish onion, chopped		
2	celery stalks, chopped	1	(28-ounce) can whole tomatoes, drained and diced
2	leeks, chopped		
2	teaspoons dried rosemary	8	cups Basic Vegetable Stock (page 223) or mineral water
2	bay leaves		
1	teaspoon kosher salt	3	cups heavy cream
½	teaspoon ground black pepper	7	garlic cloves, peeled
¼	teaspoon cayenne	¼	cup chopped chives

1. Melt the butter in a large stockpot over medium heat. Add the onion, celery, and leeks and sweat for 4 minutes, until tender.

2. Add the rosemary, bay leaves, salt, pepper, and cayenne and stir to coat the vegetables.

3. Add the lentils, tomatoes, and stock and bring the mixture to a boil. Reduce heat, partially cover, and simmer for 45 minutes, until the lentils are tender.

4. Meanwhile, combine the heavy cream and garlic cloves in a medium saucepan. Simmer for 20 minutes, until the garlic is tender and the cream is reduced by half. Remove the garlic cream from the heat and puree in a food processor or blender until smooth; set aside.

5. When the lentils are tender, stir in the pureed garlic cream. Simmer for 1 minute to heat through.

6. To serve, remove the bay leaves, ladle the soup into bowls, and top with the chopped chives.

MAKES 12 CUPS.

INDIAN BLACK LENTIL

2 tablespoons peanut oil	½ teaspoon cayenne
1 large Spanish onion, chopped	1 (28-ounce) can whole tomatoes, drained and diced
3 garlic cloves, minced	
2 tablespoons chopped fresh ginger	12 cups Basic Vegetable Stock (page 223), or mineral water
2 tablespoons sugar	
1 tablespoon Standard Garam Masala (page 235)	1 pound black lentils,* rinsed and picked over to remove debris
1½ teaspoons ground coriander seeds	1 cup plain yogurt
2 teaspoons kosher salt	½ cup chopped scallions

COOK'S NOTE:

Dal, or dried beans, are used frequently in vegetarian Indian dishes. This soup is typical of the Bengali region of India where food is usually cooked very slowly.

1. Heat the oil in a large stockpot over medium heat. Add the onion, 2 of the garlic cloves, ginger, and sugar and sauté for 10 minutes, until caramelized and golden brown.

2. Add the garam masala, coriander, salt, and cayenne and sauté for 5 minutes to cook spices.

3. Add the tomatoes and cook for 15 minutes, until the mixture becomes a thick sauce.

4. Add the stock and lentils, bring the mixture to a boil, reduce heat, partially cover, and simmer for 2 hours, until the lentils are tender.

5. Remove from heat and stir in the yogurt and reserved garlic.

6. To serve, ladle the soup into bowls and top with chopped scallions.

MAKES 10 CUPS.

* Available in Indian specialty stores and gourmet markets.

LENTIL ROASTED GARLIC

1	whole head garlic
2	tablespoons olive oil
1	large Spanish onion, chopped
2	celery stalks, chopped
2	carrots, peeled and chopped
2	teaspoons dried rosemary
2	bay leaves
1	teaspoon kosher salt
½	teaspoon ground black pepper
1	pound French lentils, rinsed and picked over to remove debris

8	cups Basic Vegetable Stock (page 223), or mineral water
1	(28-ounce) can whole tomatoes, drained and diced
3	tablespoons tomato paste
1	tablespoon balsamic vinegar
1	teaspoon minced fresh garlic
¼	cup chopped fresh Italian parsley

1. Preheat the oven to 450 degrees.
2. Wrap the whole head of garlic in foil and roast in the oven for 15 minutes, until tender. When cool enough to handle, remove the cloves from the skin and puree in a food processor or blender; set aside until ready to use.
3. Heat the oil in a large stockpot over medium heat. Add the onion, celery, and carrots and sweat for 4 minutes, until tender.
4. Add the rosemary, bay leaves, salt, and pepper and stir to coat the vegetables.
5. Add the lentils, stock, tomatoes, and tomato paste. Bring to a boil, reduce heat, partially cover, and simmer for 1 hour, until lentils are tender.
6. Stir in the pureed roasted garlic, vinegar, and fresh garlic. Simmer for 2 minutes to heat through.
7. To serve, remove the bay leaves, ladle the soup into bowls, and top with chopped parsley.

MAKES 12 CUPS.

MINESTRONE WITH LENTILS AND TOMATOES

2   tablespoons olive oil

1   large Spanish onion, chopped

2   garlic cloves, minced

2   teaspoons dried thyme leaves

2   bay leaves

1½ teaspoons kosher salt

½   teaspoon ground black pepper

½   teaspoon cayenne

10 cups Basic Vegetable Stock (page 223)

½   pound French lentils, rinsed and picked over to remove debris

2   (28-ounce) cans whole tomatoes, drained and diced

1   (3-inch) piece Parmesan cheese rind

¼   cup uncooked Arborio rice

1   head escarole, chopped

¼   cup grated Parmesan cheese

¼   cup chopped fresh Italian parsley

2   tablespoons shaved Parmesan

> **BARBER'S NOTE:**
> Shave Parmesan with a vegetable peeler for even slices.

1. Heat the oil in a large stockpot over medium heat. Add the onion and garlic and sweat for the 4 minutes, until tender.

2. Add the thyme, bay leaves, salt, pepper, and cayenne and stir to coat the vegetables.

3. Add the stock, lentils, tomatoes, and Parmesan rind and bring to a boil. Reduce heat, partially cover, and simmer for 45 minutes.

4. Stir in the rice and simmer for 20 minutes.

5. Remove from heat, stir in the escarole and grated Parmesan, cover, and let steep for 1 minute.

6. To serve, remove the bay leaves and Parmesan rind, ladle the soup into bowls, and top with the chopped parsley and shaved Parmesan.

MAKES 12 CUPS.

MOROCCAN LAMB STEW

4 tablespoons peanut oil	¼ teaspoon ground cinnamon
5 lamb shanks (about 1 pound each), cut up	6 cups Blonde Chicken Stock (page 226)
3 medium white onions, chopped	1 (28-ounce) can whole tomatoes, drained and diced
2 celery stalks, chopped	½ pound dried chickpeas (garbanzo beans), rinsed and picked over to remove debris
2 garlic cloves, sliced	
1 tablespoon minced fresh ginger	½ pound French lentils, rinsed and picked over to remove debris
2 teaspoons kosher salt	
1½ teaspoons ground coriander seeds	1 tablespoon sugar
1 teaspoon turmeric	½ cup chopped fresh cilantro
½ teaspoon ground black pepper	

1. Preheat the oven to 325 degrees.

2. Heat the oil in a large Dutch oven over medium heat. Add the lamb shanks in batches and brown on all sides. Remove the lamb from the pot with a slotted spoon, reserving the oil in the pan, and set aside.

3. Add the onions, celery, garlic, and ginger to the pot and sweat for 4 minutes, until tender.

4. Add the salt, coriander, turmeric, pepper, and cinnamon and stir to coat the vegetables.

5. Return the lamb to the pan and add 2 cups of the chicken stock, the tomatoes, and chickpeas. Bring to a boil, remove from heat, cover, and place the pot in the oven. Braise for 2 hours, until the lamb is tender. Remove the pot from the oven and remove the lamb shank pieces with a slotted spoon. Pull the lamb meat from the bone and return the meat to the pan (discard the bones or reserve for lamb stock).

6. Place the pan over medium heat and stir in the remaining 4 cups stock and lentils. Bring to a boil, reduce heat, partially cover, and simmer for 45 minutes, until the lentils are tender.

7. Stir in the sugar.

8. To serve, ladle the soup into bowls and top with the chopped cilantro.

MAKES 12 CUPS.

MULLIGATAWNY WITH LENTILS

"My favorite soup is Mulligatawny with Lentils. I found it to be a soup that should be eaten in a quiet moment, to be savored, with a glass of red wine. It is rich, aromatic, deep with feeling, hot, and spicy."—customer E-mail

1 tablespoon minced fresh ginger	6 cups Basic Vegetable Stock (page 223), or mineral water
2 garlic cloves, minced	1 pound brown lentils, rinsed and picked over to remove debris
2 tablespoons peanut oil	
1 large Spanish onion, chopped	1 cup coconut milk
¼ cup black mustard seeds*	1 bunch fresh spinach, rinsed well and chopped
1 tablespoon Standard Garam Masala (page 239)	
2 teaspoons tandoori spice mix*	1 tablespoon fresh lemon juice (optional)
2 teaspoons curry powder	1 tablespoon sugar (optional)
2 teaspoons kosher salt	½ cup chopped fresh cilantro
1 teaspoon ground cardamom seeds	
¼ teaspoon cayenne	
1 (28-ounce) can whole tomatoes, drained and diced	

1. Puree the ginger and garlic together in a blender or food processor.
2. Heat the oil in a large stockpot over medium heat. Add the onion and ginger puree and sweat for 4 minutes, until tender and golden.
3. Add the mustard seeds and cook until they begin to pop.
4. Add in the garam masala, tandoori spice mix, curry, salt, cardamom, and cayenne and stir to coat the vegetables.

*Available in gourmet food stores.

5. Add the tomatoes and simmer for 5 minutes.

6. Add the stock and lentils and bring the mixture to a boil. Reduce heat, partially cover, and simmer for 1 hour, until the lentils are tender.

7. Stir in the coconut milk and simmer for 2 minutes.

8. Remove from heat and stir in the spinach (and lemon juice and sugar if desired).

9. To serve, ladle the soup into bowls and top with chopped cilantro.

MAKES 12 CUPS.

INDIAN YELLOW SPLIT PEA

2 teaspoons Standard Garam Masala (page 235)	1 tablespoon minced fresh ginger
2 teaspoons turmeric	1 teaspoon kosher salt
1 teaspoon ground coriander	½ teaspoon cayenne
2 tablespoons peanut oil	8 cups Basic Vegetable Stock (page 223), or mineral water
1 tablespoon sugar	1 pound yellow split peas, rinsed and picked over to remove debris
1 large Spanish onion, chopped	1 teaspoon minced fresh garlic
2 celery stalks, chopped	½ cup chopped scallions
2 carrots, peeled and chopped	

1. Preheat the oven to 300 degrees.

2. Combine the garam masala, turmeric, and coriander in an oven-proof skillet. Place in the oven and dry-roast for 5 minutes. Remove from the oven and set aside until ready to use.

3. Heat the oil and sugar in a large stockpot over medium heat. Add the onion and sauté for 10 minutes until caramelized and golden brown.

4. Transfer the onions to a blender or food processor and puree until almost smooth.

5. Return the onions to the pan, add the celery and carrots, and sweat for 2 minutes.

6. Add the roasted garam masala mixture, ginger, salt, and cayenne and stir to coat the vegetables.

7. Add the stock and split peas, bring to a boil, reduce heat, partially cover, and simmer for 45 minutes, until the peas are tender.

8. Stir in the minced garlic and simmer for 2 minutes to heat through.

9. To serve, ladle the soup into bowls and top with chopped scallions.

MAKES 10 CUPS.

VEGETARIAN SPLIT PEA

2 tablespoons canola oil	½ teaspoon ground black pepper
1 large Spanish onion, chopped	1 pound green split peas, rinsed and picked over to remove debris
2 celery stalks, chopped	
2 carrots, peeled and chopped	8 cups Basic Vegetable Stock (page 223)
2 teaspoons dried thyme leaves	½ cup white wine
2 bay leaves	1 teaspoon minced fresh garlic
1 teaspoon kosher salt	¼ cup chopped fresh Italian parsley

1. Heat the oil in a large stockpot over medium heat. Add the onion, celery, and carrots and sweat for 4 minutes, until tender.

2. Add the thyme, bay leaves, salt, and pepper and stir to coat the vegetables.

3. Add the split peas, stock, and white wine, bring to a boil, reduce heat, partially cover, and simmer for 45 minutes, until the peas are tender.

4. Remove the bay leaves and puree the soup in batches in a blender or food processor until smooth.

5. Return the puree to the pot and stir in the minced garlic. Simmer for 2 minutes to heat through.

6. To serve, ladle the soup into bowls and top with chopped parsley.

MAKES 10 CUPS.

VARIATION:

SPLIT PEA WITH PANCETTA AND PARMESAN
Sauté ¼ pound of diced pancetta in butter for 10 minutes, until all the fat is rendered. Add the onion, celery, and carrots and sweat in the butter as directed (step 1). Proceed with the recipe as directed, adding ½ cup grated Parmesan to the pot with the minced garlic (step 5). Simmer for 2 minutes to heat through.

PEA PARMESAN

8	cups shelled fresh green peas, or frozen green peas	2	bay leaves
1	teaspoon sugar	6	cups Basic Vegetable Stock (page 223)
2	teaspoons kosher salt	1	(3-inch) piece Parmesan cheese rind
6	tablespoons unsalted butter	2	cups milk
1	large Spanish onion, chopped	5	tablespoons all-purpose flour
2	leeks, rinsed well and chopped	¼	teaspoon ground white pepper
2	carrots, peeled and chopped	¼	teaspoon ground nutmeg
2	teaspoons dried thyme leaves	½	cup grated Parmesan cheese
		1	teaspoon minced fresh garlic

1. Blanch the peas in rapidly boiling water for 2 minutes. Puree 6 cups of the peas with the sugar and 1 teaspoon of the salt until smooth. Set the puree and remaining whole peas aside until ready to use.

2. Melt 2 tablespoons of the butter in a large stockpot over medium heat. Add the onion, leeks, and carrots and sweat for 4 minutes, until tender.

3. Add the thyme and bay leaves and stir to coat the vegetables.

4. Add the stock and Parmesan rind and bring the mixture to a boil. Reduce heat, partially cover, and simmer for 20 minutes.

5. Meanwhile, to make the béchamel, scald the milk by heating it in a small saucepan just until bubbles appear around the edges.

6. In a separate pan, melt the remaining 4 tablespoons of the butter over low heat. Add the flour and cook until a thick, pale roux forms, stirring constantly with a wire whisk.

7. Gradually add the scalded milk, stirring constantly. Simmer until the sauce thickens and reduces by half.

8. Stir in the remaining teaspoon of salt, white pepper, and nutmeg and set aside until ready to use.

9. Stir the whole and pureed peas, béchamel, grated Parmesan, and garlic into the pot; simmer for 1 minute.

10. To serve, remove the bay leaves and Parmesan rind and ladle the soup into bowls.

MAKES 10 CUPS.

HOPPIN' JOHN PORK AND BLACK-EYED PEA

Although the directions for this recipe look fairly short, they're deceptive. Step five alone can take up to two hours, so plan an activity to keep you occupied while you wait. Why so long? The black-eyed peas need time to absorb the flavor from the pork, bacon, and vegetables. This would be a good time to change the oil in your car, do your taxes, or fertilize your lawn.

2	tablespoons peanut oil		2	bay leaves
1	(3-pound) boneless pork butt, trimmed and cut into 1-inch cubes		2	teaspoons kosher salt
			½	teaspoon ground black pepper
¼	pound slab bacon, cut into ¼-inch cubes		6	cups Blonde Chicken Stock (page 226) or mineral water
1	large Spanish onion, chopped		1	pound black-eyed peas, rinsed and picked over to remove debris
2	celery stalks, chopped			
2	carrots, peeled and chopped		¼	cup uncooked white rice
2	garlic cloves, minced		1	bunch mustard greens, chopped
2	teaspoons dried thyme leaves		½	cup chopped scallions

1. Heat the oil in a large stockpot over medium heat. Add the pork and brown on all sides. Remove the pork with a slotted spoon, reserving the oil in the pan, and set aside.

2. Add the bacon to the pot and sauté for 10 minutes, until browned and fat is rendered.

3. Add the onion, celery, carrots, and garlic and sweat for 4 minutes until tender.

4. Add the thyme, bay leaves, salt, and pepper and stir to coat the vegetables.

5. Return the pork to the pan and stir in the stock and black-eyed peas. Bring to a boil, reduce heat, partially cover, and simmer for 1 to 2 hours, until the peas are tender.
6. Add the rice and simmer for 20 minutes.
7. Remove from heat and stir in the mustard greens.
8. To serve, remove the bay leaves, ladle the soup into bowls, and top with the chopped scallions.

MAKES 12 CUPS.

NUT

NUTS ARE FREQUENTLY used in West African, Middle East-
ern, and Southeast Asian cuisine. The role of nuts varies, depending on when
you add them. When they're added to soup at the beginning, they act as
sponges by soaking up the flavors of the spices and broth. When added
halfway through cooking, nuts blend with other ingredients and pick up some
additional flavor while maintaining their strong, nutty taste. And, when you
add them at the end, nuts stay crunchy, making them an ideal garnish. Additionally, nut purees can be used at any time in the cooking process to thicken
soup.

Peanuts are the most beloved of all nuts (they're actually legumes, but
how would pea-legume butter sound?). Because of their unique flavor, peanuts
are addictive. They bring out the passion in people. Peanut people hunt down
peanuts in everything—ice cream, cookies, candy, and, as we've discovered,
soup. Add peanuts to anything and the peanut people will follow. And,
although peanuts have a strong flavor, they mellow out and complement other
ingredients when used in soups.

Almonds, walnuts, pecans, and cashews are also excellent additions to
soup, although they lack the peanut's cultlike following. Simmering almonds

in cream creates a rich, almond-scented, velvet cream—perfect for Indian-inspired soups (Mulligatawny, page 151). Walnuts have an earthy, meaty quality, and they maintain their crunch in fruit soups (Carrot, Orange, and Walnut, page 177). Pecans have a distinct, almost fruity flavor and they work especially well in Cajun soups. Cashews are the caviar of nuts, and they're always the first to disappear from any cocktail mix (an embarrassing situation for the Brazil nut—who is ultimately left sitting alone in the bowl). Not relegated to cocktail parties, cashews also add star quality to soup (Brazilian Chicken Stew, page 147).

One of our more popular soups, White Gazpacho (page 153), has an interesting history. The original white gazpacho, made with cucumbers and heavy cream, was created in Spain hundreds of years ago. The story is: Cream was often unobtainable for peasant cooks, so in order to enjoy this smooth, refreshing soup, they used almond purees to achieve the same creamy base. Whatever the origin, we love the almond flavor in this wonderful, cold summer soup.

Our Brazilian Chicken Stew has a hint of crunchy nuts, but our customers can never quite figure out which nut we use. The secret is out—we use cashews because they absorb the flavor of chilies, onion, and garlic while maintaining their rich, buttery flavor.

BRAZILIAN CHICKEN STEW

4 tablespoons peanut oil	2 teaspoons kosher salt
1 whole chicken (about 4 pounds), cut up (see page 14)	2 green bell peppers, seeded and chopped
10 cups mineral or filtered water	2 red bell peppers, seeded and chopped
1 large Spanish onion, chopped	1½ cups salted cashews
2 garlic cloves, minced	¼ cup plain bread crumbs
1 tablespoon minced fresh ginger	1 cup coconut milk
2 Pickled Jalapeños (page 237)	½ cup chopped fresh cilantro
1 (28-ounce) can whole tomatoes, drained	1 tablespoon fresh lemon juice
2 tablespoons sugar	½ teaspoon habañero pepper sauce
	5 cups cooked white rice

1. Heat 2 tablespoons of oil in a large stockpot over medium heat. Add the chicken pieces and brown on all sides. Add the water, bring to a boil, reduce heat, and simmer for 10 minutes, until the chicken is cooked through. Remove the chicken with a slotted spoon, reserve the poaching liquid, and when cool enough to handle remove the meat from the bones and set aside. Strain the poaching liquid to remove solids, reserving 8 cups, and set aside.*

2. In a blender or food processor, puree the onion, garlic, ginger, jalapeños, and tomatoes.

3. Heat the remaining 2 tablespoons of oil in a large stockpot over medium heat. Add the onion puree and sweat for 4 minutes.

4. Add the sugar and salt and stir to coat.

5. Add the bell peppers and poaching liquid and bring the mixture to a boil. Reduce heat, partially cover, and simmer for 20 minutes.

*To de-fat the stock, refrigerate for 1 hour, until a fat layer forms on the surface. Skim the layer of fat off the top and discard.

6. Meanwhile, in a blender or food processor, puree 1 cup of the cashews and the bread crumbs.

7. Stir the mixture into the soup and simmer for 2 minutes to heat through.

8. Stir in the remaining ½ cup of cashews, coconut milk, cilantro, lemon juice, and habañero sauce.

9. To serve, spoon cooked the rice into shallow bowls and ladle the soup over the top.

MAKES 12 CUPS.

MALAYSIAN CABBAGE AND PEANUT

2	heads Napa cabbage, quartered		1	teaspoon turmeric
4	tablespoons soy sauce		¼	teaspoon cayenne
2	tablespoons fresh lemon or lime juice		1	28-ounce can whole tomatoes, drained and diced
3	teaspoons kosher salt		6	cups mineral or filtered water
¼	teaspoon ground black pepper		1	medium Idaho potato, peeled, halved lengthwise, and cut into 1-inch cubes
1	pound dry roasted peanuts		2	medium sweet potatoes, peeled, halved lengthwise, and cut into 1-inch cubes
2	garlic cloves			
1	tablespoon minced fresh ginger		2	tablespoons Thai fish sauce*
2	tablespoons peanut oil		1	teaspoon Sriracha hot pepper sauce* (optional)
1	large Spanish onion, chopped			
1	tablespoon sugar			
2	teaspoons curry powder			
2	teaspoons ground coriander seeds			

1. Combine the cabbage, 2 tablespoons of the soy sauce, 1 tablespoon of the lemon juice, 1 teaspoon of the salt, and pepper in a shallow baking dish; turn to coat the cabbage. Refrigerate for 30 minutes.

2. Preheat an outdoor grill, stove-top grill pan, or broiler.

3. Grill or broil cabbage until lightly charred on all sides (about 2 to 3 minutes per side). Cut into 1-inch pieces and set aside.

4. Chop ½ cup of the peanuts into small pieces and set aside to use as garnish. Puree the remaining peanuts in a blender or food processor until a thick paste forms; set aside.

5. Puree the garlic and ginger in a blender or food processor.

*Thai fish sauce is available at Asian specialty stores and gourmet markets (see Ingredient Index, page 240).

6. Heat the oil in a large stockpot over medium heat. Add the garlic puree, onion, and sugar and sweat for 4 minutes, until tender and golden.

7. Add the curry, coriander, turmeric, remaining salt, and cayenne and stir to coat the vegetables.

8. Add the tomatoes and simmer 5 minutes.

9. Add the water, potatoes, remaining soy sauce, and fish sauce. Bring to a boil, reduce heat, and simmer for 20 minutes.

10. Stir in the grilled cabbage, pureed peanuts, remaining lemon juice, and hot pepper sauce and simmer for 2 minutes.

11. To serve, ladle the soup into bowls and top with reserved chopped peanuts.

MAKES 12 CUPS.

MULLIGATAWNY

1	tablespoon minced fresh ginger	¼	teaspoon cayenne
2	garlic cloves, minced	1	(28-ounce) can whole tomatoes, drained and diced
2	tablespoons peanut oil	6	cups Basic Vegetable Stock (page 223)
1	large Spanish onion, chopped	6	medium Idaho potatoes, peeled, halved lengthwise, and cut into 1-inch cubes
1	tablespoon sugar		
1	tablespoon Standard Garam Masala (page 235)	1	cup heavy cream
2	teaspoons ground coriander seeds	1	cup sliced almonds, lightly toasted*
2	teaspoons kosher salt	15	saffron threads
1	teaspoon turmeric	½	cup chopped scallions

1. Puree the ginger and garlic together in a blender or food processor.

2. Heat the oil in a large stockpot over medium heat. Add the onion and ginger puree and sauté for 4 minutes, until tender and golden brown.

3. Add the sugar, garam masala, coriander, salt, turmeric, and cayenne and stir to coat the vegetables. Sauté for 2 minutes to cook the spices.

4. Add the tomatoes and simmer for 5 minutes.

5. Add the stock and potatoes and bring the mixture to a boil. Reduce heat, partially cover, and simmer for 20 minutes, until the potatoes are tender.

6. Meanwhile, combine the heavy cream, half of the almonds, and the saffron in a small saucepan over medium heat. Simmer until the liquid is reduced by half.

7. Puree the almond and cream mixture in a blender until smooth.

8. Stir the almond cream into the soup and simmer for 2 minutes.

9. Stir in ¼ cup of the remaining almonds.

10. To serve, ladle the soup into bowls and top with the remaining ¼ cup of almonds and chopped scallions.

MAKES 12 CUPS.

COOK'S NOTE:

At Daily Soup, we cook raw spices until they become fragrant, to ensure that the full power of each spice is infused into the broth (see "Working with Fresh Herbs and Spices," page 13).

*To toast almonds, spread them out on baking sheet and bake at 350 degrees for 5 minutes, until golden brown.

SENEGALESE PEANUT

VARIATION:

SENEGALESE PEANUT SOUP WITH CHICKEN
Poach 1 pound boneless, skinless chicken breasts in gently simmering water for 10 minutes. Drain and when cool enough to handle, cut into 2-inch cubes. Add to the soup with the scallions, heavy cream, and garlic (step 5). Simmer for 2 minutes to heat through.

1	pound dry roasted, salted peanuts	½	teaspoon cayenne
2	tablespoons peanut oil	½	teaspoon kosher salt
1	large Spanish onion, chopped	1	(28-ounce) can whole tomatoes, drained and diced
2	celery stalks, chopped		
2	leeks, rinsed well and chopped	6	cups mineral or filtered water
2	teaspoons sugar	½	cup chopped scallions
2	teaspoons curry powder	½	cup heavy cream
2	teaspoons ground cumin	1	teaspoon minced fresh garlic

1. Chop ½ cup of the peanuts into small pieces and set aside to use as garnish. Puree the remaining peanuts in a blender or food processor until a thick paste forms; set aside.

2. Heat the oil in a large stockpot over medium heat. Add the onion, celery, and leeks and sweat for 4 minutes, until tender.

3. Add the sugar, curry, cumin, cayenne, and salt and stir to coat the vegetables.

4. Add the tomatoes, water, and peanut paste. Bring to a boil, reduce heat, and simmer for 1 hour.

5. Stir in the scallions, heavy cream, and garlic and simmer for 2 minutes to heat through.

6. To serve, ladle the soup into bowls and top with reserved chopped peanuts.

MAKES 10 CUPS.

WHITE GAZPACHO WITH ALMONDS AND GRAPES

2½ cups (about 8 ounces) blanched, sliced almonds, lightly toasted*

¼ cup fresh bread crumbs (made from day-old bread—crusts removed)

2 garlic cloves

2 tablespoons sugar

2½ teaspoons kosher salt

1 large cucumber, peeled, seeded (seeds reserved), and cut into ¼-inch cubes

2½ tablespoons sherry vinegar

¾ cup olive oil

3 cups mineral or filtered water

½ pound seedless red grapes, thinly sliced (about 2 cups sliced)

½ pound seedless green grapes, thinly sliced (about 2 cups sliced)

½ cup thinly sliced red onion

½ cup chopped scallions

1. In a blender or food processor, combine 2 cups of the almonds, bread crumbs, garlic, sugar, and salt. Process until the almonds are finely ground.

2. Add the cucumber seeds and vinegar and puree until smooth.

3. With the motor running, gradually add the oil in a thin stream. Process until smooth and thick.

4. Gradually add 2 cups of the water and puree until smooth.

5. Transfer the mixture to a large bowl and stir in the cubed cucumber, remaining cup of water, remaining ½ cup of almonds, grapes, and red onion.

6. Refrigerate until ready to serve.

7. To serve, ladle the soup into bowls and top with the chopped scallions.

MAKES 10 CUPS.

*To toast almonds, spread out on baking sheet and bake at 350 degrees for 5 minutes, until golden brown.

COCONUT

IT'S COMMON IN southern India and many parts of Southeast Asia to use grated coconut and coconut milk in stews, soups, and curries. In the United States, we use coconut almost exclusively in candy bars, desserts, and frostings. We've been a little misdirected in this country. The coconut is sweet, but not too sweet, and it pairs perfectly with spices.

We recommend using dried, unsweetened coconut for its intense flavor. Although great for piña coladas, sweetened dried coconut and sweet coconut milk are not suitable for soup. You can usually find unsweetened products in gourmet markets, health food stores, and Asian specialty shops. Lightly toasting unsweetened coconut enhances its flavor (a secret the Good Humor Man has known for years).

Coconut milk is an ideal, nonanimal-based substitute for heavy cream. The result is the same—a rich, velvety consistency with an added bonus of coconut flavor. Plus, coconut milk adds body to Asian soups while keeping them vegetarian. Coconut milk is very sensitive to high heat, so it should be added to hot soups just before serving. This will also preserve the powerful, yet delicate coconut flavor.

The "coconut milk" found inside the coconut is not really milk, it's water.

Store-bought coconut milk is made by simmering the grated white meat of the coconut in its own natural water. Once the potion cools, it's drained through cheesecloth, and then the meat is squeezed and kneaded until dry. The drained liquid sits until cream rises to the top, and then the cream is skimmed off. Sometimes the kneaded, dried solids are returned to the cream to make it thicker. Thankfully, this long and arduous process has been done for us by the folks in Thailand who package up the milk in decorative cans.

Asian cuisines vary widely in their use of ingredients, but coconut is the one constant that's used all over the region. Burmese cuisine often begins with pureed and sautéed garlic, ginger, onions, and shrimp paste. Thai cuisine is perfumed with lemongrass, dried fish, and a variety of hot chilies. Cooks in these Southeast Asian countries make use of fresh herbs, such as Thai basil, Kaffir lime leaves, and fresh coriander (cilantro). All of these fresh ingredients melt into coconut milk to create an extraordinary balance of flavors.

BAHIAN SEAFOOD STEW

2   large Spanish onions, chopped
1   habañero chile pepper, halved and seeded
2   garlic cloves
1   cup dried shrimp*
2   tablespoons peanut oil
¼   teaspoon achiote paste*
4   cups mineral or filtered water
2   (28-ounce) cans whole tomatoes, drained and diced
2   green bell peppers, seeded and chopped
2   red bell peppers, seeded and chopped

1   tablespoon fresh lemon juice
1   tablespoon fresh lime juice
1   teaspoon kosher salt
½   teaspoon ground black pepper
¼   teaspoon cayenne
1   pound medium shrimp, peeled and deveined
½   pound cod or monkfish fillet, cut into 1-inch cubes
½   pound lump crabmeat
1   cup unsweetened coconut milk
¼   cup chopped fresh cilantro
4   cups cooked rice

1. Puree the onion, habañero pepper, garlic, and dried shrimp in a blender or food processor until smooth.

2. Heat the oil and achiote paste in a large stockpot over medium heat. Add the pureed onion mixture and sauté for 2 minutes, until tender but not browned.

3. Add the water, tomatoes, bell peppers, lemon and lime juices, salt, pepper, and cayenne. Bring to a boil, reduce heat, and simmer for 15 minutes.

4. Stir in the shrimp, cod, crabmeat, coconut milk, and cilantro and simmer for 3 minutes, until the fish is cooked through.

5. To serve, spoon the rice into the bottom of soup bowls and ladle the stew over the top.

MAKES 10 CUPS.

*Dried shrimp and achiote paste are available at specialty food stores or by mail order (see Ingredient Sources, page 245).

BURMESE SHRIMP CURRY

1 large Spanish onion, chopped

3 garlic cloves, minced

1 tablespoon minced fresh ginger

2 teaspoons Thai curry paste*

2 teaspoons shrimp paste*

2 teaspoons kosher salt

1 tablespoon peanut oil

1 tablespoon dark sesame oil

1 teaspoon turmeric

1 (28-ounce) can whole tomatoes, drained and diced

6 cups Basic Vegetable Stock (page 223)

1 medium Idaho potato, peeled, halved lengthwise, and cut into 1-inch cubes

½ cup grated unsweetened coconut, lightly toasted

1 cup sliced fresh okra

1 pound medium shrimp, peeled and deveined

1 cup unsweetened coconut milk

½ cup chopped fresh cilantro

1 tablespoon sugar (optional)

1 teaspoon Sriracha hot pepper sauce* (optional)

½ cup chopped scallions

1. Puree the onion, 2 cloves of the garlic, ginger, curry paste, shrimp paste, and salt in a blender or food processor; set aside.

2. Heat the oils together in a large stockpot over medium heat. Add the onion puree and sweat for 5 minutes, until tender and golden brown.

3. Add the turmeric and simmer until the mixture forms a thick paste.

4. Add the tomatoes and simmer for 5 minutes.

5. Add the stock and potatoes and bring the mixture to a boil. Reduce heat, partially cover, and simmer for 20 minutes.

6. Add the grated coconut and okra and simmer for 5 minutes.

*Thai curry paste, shrimp paste, and Sriracha hot pepper sauce are available at Asian specialty food stores or by mail order (page 245).

7. Add the shrimp and coconut milk and simmer for 3 minutes, until the shrimp are bright red and cooked through.

8. Remove from heat and stir in the remaining garlic clove and cilantro (and sugar and hot pepper sauce if desired).

9. To serve, ladle the soup into bowls and top with the chopped scallions.

MAKES 12 CUPS.

THAI CHICKEN WITH GINGER AND COCONUT

4 tablespoons peanut oil

1 whole chicken (about 4 pounds), cut up (see page 14)

8 cups mineral or filtered water

2 garlic cloves, minced

1 tablespoon minced fresh ginger

1 (4-inch) piece lemongrass, diced

1 tablespoon sugar

2 teaspoons Thai curry paste*

2 teaspoons kosher salt

3 shallots, thinly sliced

1 (28-ounce) can whole tomatoes, drained and diced

3 medium Idaho potatoes, peeled, halved lengthwise, and cut into 1-inch cubes

1 cup unsweetened coconut milk

½ cup grated unsweetened coconut, lightly toasted

2 tablespoons finely minced Kaffir lime leaves†

1 teaspoon Sriracha hot pepper sauce*(optional)

1 bunch Chinese or regular watercress, chopped

½ cup scallions, sliced on the bias, very thin

1. Heat 2 tablespoons of the oil in a large stockpot over medium heat. Add the chicken pieces and brown on all sides. Add the water, bring to a boil, reduce heat, and simmer for 10 minutes, until the chicken is cooked through. Remove the chicken with a slotted spoon, reserve the poaching liquid, and when cool enough to handle remove the meat from the bones and set aside. Strain the poaching liquid to remove solids, reserve 6 cups stock, and set aside.**

*Thai curry paste is available at Asian specialty food stores or by mail order (page 245).

†Kaffir lime leaves can be found in specialty food stores. If they are not available, use grated lime zest or lemongrass.

**To de-fat the stock, refrigerate for 1 hour, until a fat layer forms on the surface. Skim the layer of fat off the top and discard.

2. Puree the garlic, ginger, lemongrass, sugar, curry paste, and salt in a blender or food processor.

3. Heat the remaining 2 tablespoons of oil in a large stockpot over medium heat. Add the garlic puree and shallots and sweat for 4 minutes, until tender and golden.

4. Add the tomatoes and simmer for 5 minutes.

5. Add the reserved chicken, poaching liquid, and potatoes and bring the mixture to a boil. Reduce heat, partially cover, and simmer for 20 minutes.

6. Stir in the coconut milk, toasted coconut, lime leaves, and hot sauce and simmer for 2 minutes.

7. Remove from heat and stir in the watercress.

8. To serve, ladle the soup into bowls and top with chopped scallions.

MAKES 12 CUPS.

CHICKEN WITH COCONUT

VARIATION:

INDIAN SHRIMP AND COCONUT

Use Basic Vegetable Stock (see page 223) in place of chicken stock when simmering the spices and vegetables (step 6). Add 1 pound of peeled and deveined medium shrimp when you add the coconut milk, heavy cream, and toasted coconut (step 7). Simmer for 3 minutes, until the shrimp are bright red and cooked through. Stir in the chopped tomato (step 8) and serve as directed.

"Sometimes when I'm in Russia, I can go all week without talking to the office, but keep in close touch by E-mail. For all the things you can do with E-mail, one of my favorites is getting the Daily Soup menu from a little soup shop around the corner from my office in New York. Because it arrives daily in my electronic mailbox, I receive it wherever I am. It's a lot of fun to sit in a snowstorm in, say, Gdansk, Poland, and know that back home the special of the day is Chicken with Coconut—$5.95."—Ester Dyson from her book, Release 2.0.

4 tablespoons peanut oil	2 teaspoons kosher salt
1 whole chicken (about 4 pounds), cut up (see page 14)	¼ teaspoon cayenne
10 cups mineral or filtered water	1 (28-ounce) can whole tomatoes, drained and diced
1 tablespoon minced fresh ginger	1 cup coconut milk
2 garlic cloves, minced	1 cup heavy cream
1 large Spanish onion, chopped	1 cup unsweetened, grated coconut, lightly toasted
2 tablespoons sugar	1 large, ripe beefsteak tomato, diced
1 tablespoon Standard Garam Masala (page 235)	½ cup chopped scallions
2 teaspoons ground coriander seeds	

1. Heat 2 tablespoons of the oil in a large stockpot over medium heat. Add the chicken pieces and brown on all sides. Add the water, bring to a boil, reduce heat, and simmer for 10 minutes, until the chicken is cooked through. Remove the chicken with a slotted spoon, reserve the poaching liquid, and when cool enough to handle remove the meat from the bones and set aside. Strain the poaching liquid to remove solids, reserving 8 cups, and set aside.*

*To de-fat the stock, refrigerate for 1 hour, until a fat layer forms on the surface. Skim the layer of fat off the top and discard.

2. Puree the ginger and garlic together in a blender or food processor.

3. Heat the remaining 2 tablespoons of the oil in a large stockpot over medium heat. Add the chopped onion and ginger puree and sauté for 4 minutes, until tender and golden brown.

4. Add the sugar, garam masala, coriander, salt, and cayenne and stir to coat the vegetables. Sauté for 2 minutes to cook the spices.

5. Add the canned tomatoes and simmer for 5 minutes.

6. Add the reserved chicken and poaching liquid and bring the mixture to a boil. Reduce heat, partially cover, and simmer for 20 minutes.

7. Reduce heat to low, stir in the coconut milk, heavy cream, and toasted coconut and simmer for 2 minutes.

8. Remove from heat and stir in the chopped tomato.

9. To serve, ladle the soup into bowls and top with the chopped scallions.

MAKES 12 CUPS.

CHEESE

CREAM AND CHEESE sauces are the easiest sauces to make. In fact, the most simple sauce is made by reducing wine or broth, and then adding a little cream or cheese. The same holds true for soup. In fact (pardon our French training), cream and cheese can fix almost any tasteless soup or sauce. Cheese adds two distinct qualities to soup—a sharp accent and a smooth finish. And, we use different varieties of cheese depending on the desired flavor, consistency, and ethnic origin of the soup.

Parmigiano-Reggiano is probably the finest cheese for soup because of its pungent flavor and desirable cooking characteristics. It takes 148 gallons of Holstein cow milk to produce 4 gallons of Parmigiano cheese—now that's rich cheese! Making Parmigiano is a painstaking task in which all components of the whey are removed. During this process, almost all of the water is also removed—that's why grated Parmigiano cheese never gets stringy. We use leftover Parmigiano-Reggiano rinds to infuse cheese flavor into several of our Italian vegetable soups, and we add it to our Basic Vegetable Stock (page 223) to make a Parmesan stock. You can never fully extract all of the flavor from a rind, and technically it can be used more than once. Most cheese stores discard the rinds, but climbing into their dumpster could be embarrassing, so ask your local cheese purveyor, in advance, if you can have their leftovers.

Great "soup-cheese" is one with a high cream content, because the cream prevents the cheese from clumping. Some examples include Roquefort, Gorgonzola, Muenster, Camembert, and Brie. These well-ripened cheeses undergo a lengthy fermentation process and much of their protein is broken down. The degraded proteins can tolerate higher temperatures and the cheese melts without becoming stringy.

Pressed, uncooked cheeses, like cheddar and Gouda, have a tendency to coagulate because the fat and water separate when exposed to high heat. The result is stringy globs of cheese in soup (no, you can't pass those globs off as dumplings, but you *can* fish them out and serve them with crackers at your next cocktail party). To prevent coagulation, gradually stir grated cheese into simmering soup just before serving. If the soup recipe has cream, melt the cheese in the cream first and then add the mixture to the pot.

High-fat cheeses, such as mozzarella and Mexican Queso Blanco, often melt unevenly, making them more suitable for cold soups and garnishes.

VEGETARIAN

ALPINE CHEESE

One of our first employees, Greg Johnson, loves soup, as he does many other types of food. He cooked soup for us for two years, and he had seen it all. One day, Alpine Cheese appeared on the menu. Greg didn't know what it was, so he sampled it. He went crazy. The soup spoke to him—it was a revelation. We moved him out front to tell the customers about it. We sold out in minutes.

COOK'S NOTE:
At Daily Soup, we puree this soup *just until* it's smooth, to prevent the mixture from becoming gummy. We've found that a hand-held immersion blender is the best way to create a smooth texture.

2	tablespoons unsalted butter	2	bay leaves
1	large Spanish onion, chopped	½	teaspoon ground black pepper
2	leeks, rinsed well and chopped	2	cups crumbled Gorgonzola cheese
3	carrots, peeled and chopped	½	cup heavy cream
8	medium Idaho potatoes, peeled, halved lengthwise, and cut into 1-inch cubes	1	tablespoon brandy
		1	teaspoon minced fresh garlic
6	cups Basic Vegetable Stock (page 223)	½	cup chopped scallions
2	teaspoons dried thyme leaves		

1. Melt the butter in a large stockpot over medium heat. Add the onion, leeks, and carrots and sweat for 4 minutes, until tender.
2. Add the potatoes, stock, thyme, bay leaves, and pepper. Bring to a boil, reduce heat, partially cover, and simmer for 20 minutes, until the potatoes are tender.
3. Remove the bay leaves and stir in the cheese and heavy cream.
4. Puree about one quarter of the soup in a blender or food processor until smooth.
5. Return the puree to the pot, stir in the brandy and garlic, and simmer for 2 minutes to heat through.
6. To serve, ladle the soup into bowls and top with chopped scallions.

MAKES 12 CUPS.

BUTTERNUT SQUASH WITH PARMESAN

2   tablespoons unsalted butter
1   large Spanish onion, chopped
2   celery stalks, chopped
6   cups Basic Vegetable Stock (page 223)
1   (3-inch) piece Parmesan cheese rind
2   bay leaves
2   butternut squash (about 1½ pounds each), peeled, seeded, and chopped into 1-inch cubes

2   tablespoons grated Parmesan cheese
3   fresh sage leaves, diced
1   teaspoon kosher salt
¼   teaspoon ground nutmeg
¼   teaspoon ground black pepper
⅛   teaspoon cayenne
¼   cup chopped fresh Italian parsley

1. Melt the butter in a large stockpot over medium heat. Add the onion and celery and sweat until tender, about 4 minutes.

2. Add the stock, Parmesan rind, and bay leaves and bring to a boil. Reduce heat, partially cover, and simmer for 15 minutes.

3. Add the squash and simmer, uncovered, for 20 minutes, until the squash is tender.

4. Remove the Parmesan rind and bay leaves; reserve the rind for another use.

5. Puree about one quarter of the soup in a food processor or blender until smooth.

6. Return the puree to the pot and stir in the grated Parmesan, sage, salt, nutmeg, pepper, and cayenne. Simmer for 2 minutes to heat through.

7. To serve, ladle the soup into bowls and top with chopped parsley.

MAKES 10 CUPS.

CHEDDAR CHEESE WITH POTATOES AND BACON

¼ pound slab bacon, cut into ¼-inch cubes

1 large Spanish onion, chopped

2 teaspoons dried thyme leaves

2 bay leaves

8 medium Idaho potatoes, peeled, halved lengthwise, and cut into 1-inch cubes

6 cups Basic Vegetable Stock (page 223)

2 cups grated extra-sharp cheddar cheese

½ cup heavy cream

1 teaspoon minced fresh garlic

½ teaspoon kosher salt

½ teaspoon ground black pepper

½ cup chopped scallions

CHEESE CURDLER'S NOTE:
Cheddar cheese has a tendency to clump and coagulate when it's added to hot liquid. After adding cheddar, do not allow the soup to boil, and serve as soon as possible.

1. Cook the bacon in a large stockpot over medium heat until golden brown. Remove half of the bacon with a slotted spoon and set aside to use as garnish.

2. Add the onion to the pot and sweat for 4 minutes, until tender.

3. Add the thyme and bay leaves and stir to coat the onion.

4. Add the potatoes and stock and bring the mixture to a boil. Reduce heat, partially cover, and simmer for 20 minutes, until the potatoes are tender.

5. Stir in the cheese and heavy cream and heat through.

6. Remove the bay leaves and puree about one quarter of the soup in a blender or food processor until smooth.

7. Return the puree to the pot and stir in the garlic, salt, and pepper. Simmer for 1 minute to heat through.

8. To serve, ladle the soup into bowls and top with the chopped scallions and reserved bacon.

MAKES 10 CUPS.

CHICKPEAS, PENNE, AND GORGONZOLA

½ **pound dried chickpeas (garbanzo beans)**
2 **tablespoons olive oil**
3 **medium white onions, chopped**
2 **celery stalks, chopped**
2 **leeks, rinsed well and chopped**
3 **garlic cloves, minced**
1 **bunch fresh rosemary, leaves chopped, stems reserved**
2 **bay leaves**
1 **teaspoon kosher salt**

½ **teaspoon ground black pepper**
⅛ **teaspoon cayenne**
8 **cups Basic Vegetable Stock (page 223), or mineral water**
1 **cup uncooked penne pasta**
1 **cup crumbled Gorgonzola cheese**
1 **bunch spinach, rinsed well and chopped**
1 **tablespoon balsamic vinegar**
½ **cup chopped scallions**

1. Drain the chickpeas, rinse under cold water, and set aside.
2. Heat the oil in a large stockpot over medium heat. Add the onions, celery, leeks, and 2 garlic cloves. Sweat for 4 minutes, until tender.
3. Tie the rosemary stems together with string and add to the pot with the bay leaves, salt, pepper, and cayenne; stir to coat the vegetables.
4. Add the chickpeas and stock and bring to a boil. Reduce heat, partially cover, and simmer for 1 hour.
5. Add the penne and cook for 7 minutes, until tender.
6. Stir in the cheese and simmer for 2 minutes, until the cheese melts.
7. Remove from heat, remove the rosemary stems, and stir in the reserved rosemary leaves, spinach, balsamic vinegar and remaining garlic clove. Cover and let steep for 1 minute.
8. To serve, ladle the soup into bowls and top with chopped scallions.

MAKES 12 CUPS.

MEXICAN CHEESE

One of the key ingredients in this soup is epazote, a wild herb that resembles oregano. We honestly didn't know about this ingredient when we first developed the soup, let alone that it was a known "carminitive" (it reduces gas). Javier, one of our cooks, is Mexican, and he turned us on to epazote when he brought it back from a vacation with his family in Mexico. We still tease him about smuggling epazote into the United States.

2 tablespoons peanut oil	6 cups Basic Vegetable Stock (page 223)
3 medium white onions, chopped	1 (28-ounce) can whole tomatoes, drained and diced
1 chipotle chile in adobo, with ½ teaspoon sauce, minced*	2½ cups grated Queso Blanco* or Monterey Jack cheese
1 teaspoon dried, ground epazote*	½ cup crumbled feta cheese
1 avocado leaf*	½ cup heavy cream
1 teaspoon kosher salt	½ cup chopped fresh cilantro
8 red bliss potatoes, cut into 1-inch cubes	1 teaspoon minced fresh garlic

1. Heat the oil in a large stockpot over medium heat. Add the onions and sweat for 4 minutes, until tender.

2. Add the chipotle in adobo with sauce, epazote, avocado leaf, and salt and stir to coat the vegetables.

3. Add the potatoes, stock, and tomatoes, bring to a boil, reduce heat, partially cover, and simmer for 20 minutes, until the potatoes are tender.

4. Stir in 2 cups of the Queso Blanco, the feta, and heavy cream and simmer for 2 minutes, until cheese melts.

*Available in Mexican specialty stores, or by mail order (page 245).

5. Remove the avocado leaf and puree about one quarter of the soup in a blender or food processor until smooth.

6. Return the puree to the pan, stir in the cilantro and garlic, and simmer for 2 minutes to heat through.

7. To serve, ladle the soup into bowls and top with remaining the ½ cup of grated Queso Blanco cheese.

MAKES 10 CUPS.

Periodic Table of the Soups

DAILY SOUP

IA																	0
1 B	IIA											IIIA	IVA	VA	VIA	VIIA	2 Hc
3 Fo	4 Co											5 M	6 To	7 Bi	8 Ch	9 R	10 A
11 Wa	12 Mt	IIIB	IVB	VB	VIB	VIIB	——— VIII ———			IB	IIB	13 Sv	14 Tb	15 Lb	16 Ne	17 Cp	18 Mc
19 Tc	20 Yi	21 St	22 Bo	23 Ba	24 P	25 M	26 Ju	27 Vp	28 Rv	29 Be	30 Ci	31 La	32 Tf	33 Cb	34 C	35 Vg	36 Sp
37 Mc	38 Pd	39 Vs	40 Th	41 Po	42 B4	43 Sm	44 Wg	45 Bs	46 G	47 Bb	48 Cb	49 Cj	50 Tc	51 Bb	52 Pc	53 Gg	54 Ci
55 Bs	56 Bu	57 +Ci	72 Sm	73 Mr	74 Nz	75 Wi	76 Wc	77 Jp	78 Tm	79 Wb	80 Cw	81 Ce	82 Tg	83 Sb	84 Sb	85 Rg	86 Cv
87 Bi	88 Z	89 -Ms	104 Mt	105 Ci	106	107	108	109	110	111	112	113					

Row labels: 1, 2, 3, 4, 5, 6, 7

+Emulsion Series	58 Ss	59 Qw	60 In	61 Sp	62 Tm	63 Re	64 Cy	65 Sw	66 Cc	67 Vp	68 Gt	69 Tb	70 Ma	71 Lu
+Acidide Series	90 Ls	91 X	92 Re	93 Am	94 As	95 Wb	96 Sc	97 Yb	98 Sg	99 Vc	100 Ts	101 Ttb	102 Bc	103 Lr

Soup Families

IA- BROTHOGEN
IIA- CONSOMMÉ
IIIB- STOCKINE
IVB- BOUILLION
VB- BASEIUM
VIB- POTATOGEN
VIIB- MINESTRONINIUM
VIII- THE RARE EARTHS
  JUICICON
  VEGETABLE PUREE
  RAW VEGETABLE
IB- BEANIUM
IIB- CHILICON
IIIA- MEAT
IVA- TOMATOCON
VA- BISQUEIUM
VIA- CHOWDER
VIIA- ROUX
0- HEAVY CREAMIUM

FRUIT

FRUIT SOUPS ARE not just for dessert anymore. At Daily Soup, soup is a meal, therefore all of our fruit soups must fill you up. So, we can't serve Banana Bisque or Blueberry Chowder. They wouldn't be filling. They might, however, make a fine topping for ice cream.

Most of our fruit soups are served cold, so the fruit must be ripe. To counterbalance the sweetness of fruit, we add complementary ingredients such as savory spices or stocks, chicken or shellfish, and intense herbs like cilantro and mint. It becomes a three course meal in one soup: a light appetizer, a hearty main course, and a sweet dessert.

Two reasons to eat fruit soup right away:

1. The enzymes in fruit (especially papaya and pineapple) break down protein and tenderize meat, such as chicken and shellfish. The result is meat with a mealy texture.

2. Soup with raw fruit has a short shelf life because the acid from the fruit "chemically" cooks other ingredients (like vegetables and herbs) and makes them wilt.

Some of our most unusual soup creations are served chilled, and the arena of cold soup as a meal is still very much unexplored. Customers always ask,

"What are you going to do in the summer?" referring to the myth that soup isn't appropriate on hot days. We suggest they try some of our cold soups. We have a few celebrated classics, such as Gazpacho (page 43), Vichyssoise (page 96), and Borscht (page 31), but many of our cold soups contain nontraditional, exotic ingredient combinations, such as Watermelon with Grilled Chicken (page 178) and Lobster Mango with Avocado (page 180).

The basic theory behind a cold soup is to take a salad recipe and fit it into a bowl—but this only works if you understand the role of each ingredient. Most salads have an acid of some type, such as vinegar or lemon juice. Also, most salads are tossed right before serving to prevent the acid from wilting the vegetables. In cold soups, the goal is the same—to delay the reaction of the acid with the fruit and other ingredients—so once everything is blended don't waste time before digging in!

CARROT, ORANGE, AND WALNUT

8	cups mineral or filtered water	2½	teaspoons kosher salt
8	carrots, peeled and cut into 1-inch pieces	4	oranges, peeled and cut into segments
2	celery stalks, chopped	2	cups chopped walnuts
1	large Spanish onion, chopped	1	cup orange juice
1	tablespoon minced fresh ginger	2	tablespoons sugar
1	Pickled Jalapeño (page 237)	½	cup chopped scallions

1. Combine the water, carrots, celery, onion, ginger, jalapeño, and salt in a large stockpot over medium heat. Bring the mixture to a boil, reduce heat, partially cover, and simmer for 20 minutes, until the carrots are tender.

2. Puree the mixture in batches in a blender or food processor.

3. Transfer the puree to a large bowl and stir in the orange sections, walnuts, orange juice, and sugar.

4. Refrigerate until ready to serve.

5. To serve, ladle the soup into bowls and top with chopped scallions.

MAKES 10 CUPS.

WATERMELON WITH GRILLED CHICKEN

2 poblano chilies

2 teaspoons ground coriander seeds

10 cups seeded, cubed watermelon (about 10 pounds whole)

½ cup mineral or filtered water

¼ cup orange juice

2 tablespoons fresh lime juice

2 tablespoons sugar

2½ teaspoons kosher salt

1 pound boneless, skinless chicken breasts

1 tablespoon olive oil

½ teaspoon ground black pepper

½ cup chopped fresh cilantro

¼ cup chopped fresh mint

½ cup chopped scallions

1. Preheat the oven to 450 degrees.

2. Place the poblano chilies on a baking sheet and roast for 20 minutes, until charred on all sides, turning halfway through the cooking time. Remove them from the oven, place in plastic bags, and let steam for 5 minutes. Remove them from the bag, peel away the skin, halve, seed, and cut into ½-inch cubes; set aside.

3. Dry roast the coriander seeds by cooking them in a small skillet over low heat for 4 minutes.

4. In a blender or food processor, puree half of the watermelon with the water, roasted coriander seeds, orange juice, 1 tablespoon of the lime juice, sugar, and 1½ teaspoons of the salt. Transfer the mixture to a large bowl and set aside.

5. Preheat a grill pan, outdoor grill, or broiler.

6. Combine the chicken, olive oil, remaining tablespoon of lime juice, remaining teaspoon of salt, and pepper.

7. Cook the chicken on the hot grill (or 4 inches from the heat source of the

broiler) until browned on both sides and cooked through, about 4 to 5 minutes per side. Remove from heat and slice into 1-inch cubes.

8. Stir the chicken into the watermelon mixture.

9. Add the remaining watermelon cubes, poblano chilies, cilantro, and mint and mix well.

10. Refrigerate until ready to serve.

11. To serve, ladle the soup into bowls and top with the chopped scallions.

MAKES 10 CUPS.

LOBSTER MANGO WITH AVOCADO

6   mangos (about 5 pounds), peeled,
     seeded, and cut into ½-inch cubes
3   cups Basic Vegetable Stock (page
     223), or mineral water
1   Pickled Jalapeño (page 237)
2   tablespoons sugar
2½   teaspoons kosher salt

2   Haas avocados,* peeled, seeded, and
     cut into ½-inch cubes
1   tablespoon fresh lemon juice
1   pound cooked lobster meat
½   cup thinly sliced red onion
½   cup chopped fresh cilantro
½   cup chopped fresh Italian parsley

1. In a blender or food processor, puree half of the mangos with the stock, jalapeño, sugar, and 1½ teaspoons of the salt. Transfer the mixture to a large bowl and set aside.

2. Place the avocados in a small bowl with the lemon juice and remaining 1 teaspoon of salt and stir to coat.

3. Stir the mixture into the mango puree.

4. Stir in the remaining chopped mango, lobster, onion, and cilantro.

5. Refrigerate until ready to serve.

6. To serve, ladle the soup into bowls and top with parsley.

MAKES 10 CUPS.

*We like to use Haas avocados, the purplish-black variety from California. Because Haas avocados contain twice as much fat as the smaller, smooth-skin, green avocados from Florida, they have a rich and buttery flesh that is perfectly suited for our soups.

PINEAPPLE SHRIMP

1 pound medium shrimp, peeled and deveined

2 ripe pineapples, peeled, cored, and cut into 1-inch cubes

1½ cups Basic Vegetable Stock (page 223) or mineral water

1 Pickled Jalapeño (page 237)

2 tablespoons sugar

2½ teaspoons kosher salt

2 red bell peppers, seeded and cut into ½-inch pieces

½ cup thinly sliced red onion

½ cup chopped scallions

1. Cook the shrimp in a large pot of rapidly boiling water for 3 minutes, until bright red and cooked through. Rinse under cold water to prevent further cooking and set aside.

2. In a blender or food processor, puree one of the pineapples with ½ cup of the stock.

3. Add the jalapeño, sugar, and salt and process until blended.

4. Transfer the mixture to a large bowl and stir in the remaining stock, cooked shrimp, remaining pineapple, red pepper, and red onion.

5. Refrigerate until ready to serve.

6. To serve, ladle the soup into bowls and top with the chopped scallions.

MAKES 10 CUPS.

181

THAI MELON WITH PEANUTS

COOK'S NOTE:

In Thai cuisine, limes are used to balance flavors—the sour, citrus taste is often matched up with sugar in a variety of dishes. The Kaffir lime is smaller than Western limes and the firm, shiny, bright green leaves are used in Thai cooking. We like to use the leaves, too— we just pound them with a meat mallet until they're soft and then we finely mince them. If you cannot find Kaffir lime leaves, substitute lime zest or lemongrass.

2 honeydew melons, peeled, seeded, and cut into ½-inch cubes
½ cup Basic Vegetable Stock (page 223), or mineral water
2 tablespoons sugar
2½ teaspoons kosher salt
1 teaspoon green Thai curry paste*
2 garlic cloves, minced
1 tablespoon minced fresh ginger
1 tablespoon peanut oil
1 tablespoon chopped Kaffir lime leaves (or 1 teaspoon lime zest)*
2 cups dry roasted, salted peanuts
1 tablespoon fresh lime juice
½ cup chopped scallions

1. In a blender or food processor, puree half of the melon with the stock, sugar, and salt; set aside.
2. Puree the curry paste, garlic, and ginger together in a blender or food processor.
3. Heat the oil in a large skillet over medium heat. Add the curry puree and sauté 4 minutes.
4. Add the mixture to the honeydew mixture in the blender; puree until blended.
5. Add the Kaffir lime leaves and ¼ cup of the peanuts and puree until blended.
6. Transfer the mixture to a large bowl and stir in the remaining honeydew, remaining 1¾ cup peanuts, and the lime juice.
7. Refrigerate until ready to serve.
8. To serve, ladle the soup into bowls and top with the chopped scallions.

MAKES 10 CUPS.

*Available in Asian specialty stores and gourmet markets.

AVOCADO WITH GRILLED SHRIMP

1 pound medium shrimp, peeled and deveined

2 tablespoons fresh lemon juice

1 tablespoon olive oil

2½ teaspoons kosher salt

½ teaspoon ground black pepper

2 Haas avocados,* seeded and cut into ¼-inch cubes

6 beefsteak tomatoes (about 4 pounds), halved and seeded, seeds reserved

1 cup Basic Vegetable Stock (page 223)

1 Pickled Jalapeño (page 237)

2 garlic cloves

1 cup tomato juice

½ cup chopped fresh cilantro

½ cup thinly sliced red onion

½ cup chopped fresh parsley

VARIATION:

GRILLED CHICKEN AVOCADO
Substitute 1 pound boneless, skinless chicken breasts for the shrimp. Marinate as directed and grill 4 to 5 minutes per side, until cooked through. Slice into thin strips before adding to the soup.

1. In a shallow dish, combine the shrimp, 1 tablespoon of the lemon juice, olive oil, 1 teaspoon of the salt, and pepper. Let stand 5 minutes.

2. Preheat a grill, grill pan, or broiler.

3. Grill or broil the shrimp 2 minutes per side, until bright red and cooked through. Remove from heat and set aside.

4. In a small bowl, combine the avocado and remaining tablespoon lemon juice; set aside.

5. Cut half of the tomatoes into small dice and set aside.

6. In a blender or food processor, combine the remaining tomatoes, all of the tomato seeds, stock, remaining 1½ teaspoons of the salt, jalapeño, and garlic. Puree until smooth.

*We like to use Haas avocados, the purplish-black variety from California. Because Haas avocados contain twice as much fat as the smaller, smooth-skin, green avocados from Florida, they have a rich and buttery flesh that is perfectly suited for our soups.

7. Transfer the mixture to a large bowl and stir in the diced tomatoes, grilled shrimp, avocado mixture, tomato juice, cilantro, and red onion.
8. To serve, ladle the soup into bowls and top with chopped parsley.

MAKES 10 CUPS.

BEP (BLACK EYED PEA), 1½", shapely, colorful, and dry resident of Louisiana seeking fun loving, slender, popular, down to earth, **white rice,** 1–2½", to make Hoppin' John together. Request descriptive note/current photo (a must). POB 9786 ☎ ✉

FSO (FIRM SPANISH ONION), 2 weeks, 4", spicy, round, nicely layered, nonjudgmental, non-smoker, relaxed, outgoing, better when cooked, and into tennis, known to make you cry, seeking long term relationship with grain eating, attractive **chicken,** 3 months, 1½', who is independent, clever, says "bock bock," up for tons of boiling fun, and feels now is the time. Photo #53677 ☎ ✉

AKC (ALASKAN KING CRAB), 6 months, 3" (but long legs), red, has seen *Jaws* 5 times, loves poetry, sincere, and not crabby, likes to swim and dive, seeks successful, dirty, hairy, fibrous **leek** who isn't scared of a bear, for making bisque all night long. Party!! Yeah!! Please include a recent photo with your note or just bring Brandy. 0000 ✉

SGC (SINGLE GREEN CUCUMBER), 1 week, 8", shiny, funny, full of seeds, good for your skin, likes long romantic walks on moonlit beaches, and scared of dogs. Seeking juicy, nonreligious, also full of seeds, **tomato** for cuddling and making Gazpacho. No prior Spanish speaking necessary. To your note/photo, I'll reply with my bona fides and you can decide if I meet your high standards. 4657 ☎ ✉

RSB (RAW SIDE OF BEEF), 2 DAYS, 4'3", heavy but not overweight, likes grass or hay, predicts rain, clean living, articulate, Midwestern. Would like to meet good-looking, educated, non–meat eating **cumin** for long hikes or just making chili together. Must enjoy being naked (or skinless) together, photography, and desire to squeeze every ounce out of life. No picture necessary. #97681 ☎ ✉

LFP (LITTLE FRESH PEA), 1 week, ¼", cool, confident, enjoys Pavarotti, young but I'll captivate you with my charm. Searching for much older, financially stable, Italian **Parmigiano-Reggiano** with rugged good looks and an open mind to marriage, to build soup together (or just bathe). Looks are not important, but a photo couldn't hurt. Available immediately. #50998 ☎

SUCCESSFUL, LONG-STEMMED Wild Mushroom seeks family of **Barley,** 2–3, 1 cm, for Eastern European soup romance and possibly more. I am athletic, a fungus, love logs, and hate tight spaces. Only functional families need apply. Send your latest Christmas family photo. PO Box 1650, Michigan ☎ ✉

PTS (PINK TIGER SHRIMP), 3", hypnotic red stripes, Atlantic Ocean Graduate, enjoys eating plankton, nonkosher (but willing to learn) is seeking ground **Thai curry** with adventurous spirit, willingness to commit, love of sailing. Must speak 3rd grade English and be aromatic enough to make Asian soup together. Do not squander time. No photo, just drop in. #526798909577883337726 ☎ ✉

ROUX

A ROUX (ROO, not rooks) is a thickening agent used *consciously* in soup cooking.

Sometimes thickening with flour and oil is done unconsciously. For example, when you dredge a piece of chicken in flour and then sauté it in oil, the flour thickens the oil and juices from the chicken. When you add wine or stock, you get a thick sauce. Using a roux in soup is basically the same process, but the stock and roux are cooked separately.

We use a roux because it is virtually flavorless and has a silken quality second only to cream. A roux disperses both starch and fat evenly into broth and changes the consistency while enhancing the rich, complicated flavor. Used this way, it's better than cream (almost impossible), and it doesn't distract your attention from the distinct flavor of the soup.

To make a roux, equal amounts of butter or oil and flour are heated in a pan and stirred until the flour loses its *cereal* smell. A roux requires constant stirring with a wire whisk, and the mixture gets incredibly hot. A roux is second only to caramel as one of the worst kitchen burns because it sticks to your skin, like napalm.

If you notice any black specks in your roux, be sad—it's burnt. There's no way to salvage a burnt roux. The burnt flavor will dominate the soup (therefore, it's no longer a *flavorless* thickening agent). The good news is, you can try again. Adding other ingredients to the roux shocks (or cools) it, halts the cooking process, and prevents the flour from burning. With good timing, this technique can also be used as a fire extinguisher. When vegetables are cooked in a roux, a unique combination of cooking methods takes place—the vegetables are simultaneously poached, steamed, and sautéed.

In traditional French cooking, there are three types of roux. *Blonde*, the first stage; *white*, when the flour just begins to cook; and *brown*, a light caramel color that evolves after good stirring. Of these three, we use the white roux in our pot pies.

Cajun cooks have taken roux to three new levels, *reddish brown*, *dark brown*, and *very dark brown*. The stages of brown to very dark brown are used to color and thicken sauces, soups, and gumbos. A darker roux adds a toasted nut flavor and a deep, rich color. The reddish brown roux is used in étouffées and the dark brown in gumbos. If you're planning a Mardi Gras party, be advised that your guests may be too inebriated to compliment you on your various shades of roux.

The darker the roux, the less thickening power it has because the thickening properties of the starch in the flour have been broken down. More of a dark-colored roux is needed to thicken a soup than equal measures of a white roux. Also, a dark roux will "break" or separate if it gets too hot, so don't allow the soup to boil for long periods of time.

CHICKEN POT PIE

2 tablespoons peanut oil
1 whole chicken (about 4 pounds), cut up (see page 14)
10 cups mineral or filtered water
2 tablespoons unsalted butter
2 tablespoons all-purpose flour
3 medium white onions, chopped
2 celery stalks, chopped
2 carrots, peeled and chopped
½ pound button mushrooms, stems trimmed and caps sliced
2 teaspoons dried thyme leaves
2 bay leaves

2 teaspoons kosher salt
½ teaspoon ground black pepper
3 medium potatoes, peeled, halved lengthwise, and cut into 1-inch cubes
2 cups fresh shelled green peas
½ cup heavy cream

FOR THE BISCUITS:
1¾ cups all-purpose flour
2 teaspoons baking powder
1 teaspoon kosher salt
4 tablespoons unsalted butter
½ cup milk

1. Heat the oil in a large stockpot over medium heat. Add the chicken pieces and brown on all sides. Add the water, bring to a boil, reduce heat, partially cover, and simmer for 10 minutes, until the chicken is cooked through. Remove the chicken with a slotted spoon, reserve the broth, and when cool enough to handle, pull the meat from the the bones and set aside. Strain the broth to remove solids, reserving 6 cups, and set aside.*

2. Preheat the oven to 425 degrees.

3. Melt the butter with the flour in a large stockpot until thick and golden, stirring constantly with a wire whisk.

4. Add the onions, celery, carrots, and mushrooms and sweat for 4 minutes, until tender.

*To de-fat the stock, refrigerate for 1 hour, until a fat layer forms on the surface. Skim the layer of fat off the top and discard.

VARIATION:
LOBSTER POT PIE
Cook a live 2 to 3 pound lobster in a large pot of rapidly boiling water for 10 minutes. Drain and reserve 6 cups of the poaching liquid. Remove the lobster meat from the tail, body, and claws and cut into 1-inch cubes. Add the lobster meat and poaching liquid when instructed to add the chicken, chicken poaching liquid, and potatoes (step 6). Proceed with the recipe as directed. If desired, add 2 chopped leeks to the vegetable mixture (step 4).

VARIATION:
MUSHROOM POT PIE
First, make a mushroom stock—Sauté the stems from 2 pounds of mixed mushrooms

(any combination of shiitake, button, cremini, oyster, chanterelles, and black trumpet) in 2 tablespoons of butter for 5 minutes, until tender and releasing juice. Add 10 cups of mineral water and ¼ cup of port and bring the mixture to a boil. Reduce heat, partially cover, and simmer for 20 minutes. Strain the stock through a fine sieve to remove solids and reserve 6 cups of the liquid. Add sliced mushroom caps and mushroom poaching liquid when instructed to add the chicken, chicken poaching liquid, and potatoes (step 6). Proceed with the recipe as directed.

5. Add the thyme, bay leaves, salt, and pepper and stir to coat the vegetables.

6. Add the reserved poaching liquid, chicken, and potatoes and bring the mixture to a boil. Reduce heat, partially cover, and simmer for 20 minutes.

7. Add the green peas and heavy cream and simmer 2 minutes.

8. To make the crust, combine the flour, baking powder, and salt in a food processor and process until blended. Add the butter and process until the mixture resembles coarse meal. With the motor running, gradually add the milk and process until the mixture forms a dough. Turn the dough out on a lightly floured surface and roll out to ½-inch thickness. Cut ten 3-inch circles using a biscuit cutter or an upside-down glass.

9. Place the rounds on top of the soup in the pot.

10. Place the pot in the oven and bake, uncovered, for 12 minutes, until the biscuits are puffed up and golden.

11. To serve, remove the bay leaves, ladle the soup into bowls, and top with biscuits.

MAKES 12 CUPS.

VEGETABLE GUMBO

½ pound black-eyed peas, rinsed and picked over to remove debris

8 cups mineral or filtered water

2 tablespoons peanut oil

2 tablespoons all-purpose flour

1 large Spanish onion, chopped

2 celery stalks, chopped

2 green bell peppers, seeded and chopped

2 red bell peppers, seeded and chopped

2 teaspoons dried thyme leaves

2 teaspoons dried oregano

2 bay leaves

1½ teaspoons onion powder

1½ teaspoons garlic powder

1½ teaspoons mustard powder

½ teaspoon cayenne

½ teaspoon ground black pepper

½ teaspoon ground white pepper

2 teaspoons kosher salt

4 cups Basic Vegetable Stock (page 223)

2 cups tomato juice

1 butternut squash (about 1½ pounds), peeled, seeded, and cut into 1-inch cubes

3 yams, peeled, halved lengthwise, and cut into 1-inch cubes

1 cup sliced fresh okra

1 bunch kale, chopped

½ cup chopped scallions

1 teaspoon minced fresh garlic

1. Place the black-eyed peas and water in a large stockpot. Set over medium heat and bring to a boil. Reduce heat, partially cover, and simmer for 1 hour, until the peas are tender. Drain and set aside until ready to use.

2. Heat the oil and flour in a large stockpot over medium heat. Cook until the mixture forms a thick, rust-colored roux, about 5 to 7 minutes.

3. Add the onion, celery, and green and red peppers and sweat for 4 minutes, until tender.

4. Add the thyme, oregano, bay leaves, the onion, garlic, and mustard powders, the cayenne, the black and white peppers, and the salt and stir to coat the vegetables.

5. Add the stock, tomato juice, butternut squash, yams, okra, and cooked black-eyed peas and bring the mixture to a boil. Reduce heat, partially cover, and simmer for 20 minutes.

6. Remove from heat, stir in the kale, cover, and let steep for 1 minute.

7. Stir in the scallions and minced garlic.

8. To serve, remove the bay leaves and ladle the gumbo into bowls.

MAKES 12 CUPS.

GREEN GUMBO WITH OYSTERS

1½ pounds oysters, shucked, shells reserved

8 cups mineral or filtered water

4 tablespoons peanut oil

4 tablespoons all-purpose flour

1 large Spanish onion, chopped

2 celery stalks, chopped

2 green bell peppers, seeded and chopped

3 garlic cloves, minced

2 teaspoons dried thyme leaves

2 bay leaves

2 teaspoons kosher salt

1½ teaspoons onion powder

1½ teaspoons garlic powder

1½ teaspoons mustard powder

1½ teaspoons ground turmeric

½ teaspoon ground black pepper

½ teaspoon ground white pepper

½ teaspoon cayenne

1 cup sliced fresh okra

2 tablespoons filé powder

1 bunch mustard greens, chopped

½ cup chopped scallions

1. Combine the oysters, shells, and water in a large stockpot over medium heat. Bring to a boil, reduce heat, and simmer for 20 minutes. Strain the liquid to remove the solids, reserving 6 cups of the broth. Discard the shells and set the oysters aside.

2. Heat the oil with the flour in a stockpot over medium heat. Cook until a thick, rust-colored roux forms, stirring constantly with a wire whisk.

3. Add the onion, celery, green peppers, and 2 of the garlic cloves and sweat for 4 minutes, until tender.

4. Add the thyme, bay leaves, salt, the onion, garlic, and mustard powders, turmeric, the black and white peppers, and the cayenne and stir to coat the vegetables.

5. Add the okra and reserved oyster broth. Bring to a boil, reduce heat, partially cover, and simmer for 20 minutes.

6. Stir in the oysters and simmer for 2 minutes.

COOK'S NOTE:

In this recipe, we use filé powder, the powdered root of the sassafras plant, as a thickener. Once we add filé powder, we make sure the soup does *not* return to a boil—because when filé powder boils, it becomes stringy and gummy (filé is French for "stringy"—and it lives up to its name). The ideal thickness for gumbo varies, depending on who you ask. Some search for a gumbo with a gravylike consistency, while others prefer a more brothy dish. We like to serve extra filé powder on the side, for those who want a thicker broth.

7. Reduce heat to low and gradually stir in the filé powder. Simmer until the mixture thickens, stirring constantly with a wire whisk.
8. Remove from heat and stir in the mustard greens, scallions, and the remaining minced garlic. Cover and let steep 1 minute.
9. To serve, remove the bay leaves and ladle the gumbo into bowls.

MAKES 10 CUPS.

RABBIT-ANDOUILLE GUMBO

2 links (about ¾ pound) andouille sausage
12 cups mineral or filtered water
6 tablespoons peanut oil
2 pounds rabbit legs
4 tablespoons all-purpose flour
1 large Spanish onion, chopped
2 celery stalks, chopped
2 green bell peppers, seeded and chopped
2 teaspoons dried thyme leaves
2 teaspoons dried oregano

2 teaspoons kosher salt
2 bay leaves
1½ teaspoons onion powder
1½ teaspoons garlic powder
1½ teaspoons mustard powder
½ teaspoon cayenne
½ teaspoon ground black pepper
½ teaspoon ground white pepper
1 cup tomato juice
1 cup sliced fresh okra
½ cup chopped scallions
1 teaspoon minced fresh garlic

VARIATION:

SHRIMP AND ANDOUILLE GUMBO

Use chicken stock instead of rabbit stock. After simmering vegetables, spices, and andouille sausage for 20 minutes (step 6), add 1 pound of peeled and deveined medium shrimp. Simmer for 3 minutes, until the shrimp are bright red and cooked through. Proceed with the recipe as directed.

1. Combine the sausage and 6 cups of water in a medium saucepan over medium heat. Bring to a boil, reduce heat, and poach for 10 minutes. Remove the sausage with a slotted spoon, reserving 2 cups of the poaching liquid. When the sausage is cool enough to handle, slice into rounds and set aside.

2. Heat 2 tablespoons of the oil in a large stockpot over medium heat. Add the rabbit legs and brown on all sides. Add the remaining 6 cups of water, bring to a boil, reduce heat, and simmer for 10 minutes, until the rabbit is cooked through. Remove the legs from the pot with a slotted spoon, reserving 4 cups of the stock. When cool enough to handle, pull the meat from the bones and set aside (discard bones).

3. Heat the remaining 4 tablespoons of oil with the flour in the stockpot over medium heat. Cook until a thick, rust-colored roux forms, stirring constantly with a wire whisk.

4. Add the onion, celery, and green peppers and sweat for 4 minutes, until tender.

5. Add the thyme, oregano, salt, bay leaves, the onion, garlic, and mustard powders, the cayenne, and the black and white peppers and stir to coat the vegetables.

6. Add the rabbit stock, tomato juice, okra, reserved sausage and sausage poaching liquid, and reserved rabbit meat. Bring to a boil, reduce heat, partially cover, and simmer for 20 minutes.

7. Remove from heat and stir in the scallions and minced garlic.

8. To serve, remove the bay leaves and ladle the gumbo into bowls.

MAKES 12 CUPS.

CRAWFISH ÉTOUFFÉE

4	tablespoons unsalted butter	½	teaspoon ground black pepper	
4	tablespoons all-purpose flour	½	teaspoon ground white pepper	
1	tablespoon sugar	½	teaspoon cayenne	
1	large Spanish onion, chopped	6	cups Basic Shellfish Stock (page 225)	
2	celery stalks, chopped	1	(28-ounce) can whole tomatoes with tomato puree, diced	
2	teaspoons dried thyme leaves	1	pound cooked crawfish meat	
2	bay leaves	½	cup chopped fresh Italian parsley	
1½	teaspoons onion powder	2	tablespoons fresh lemon juice	
1½	teaspoons garlic powder	1	teaspoon minced fresh garlic	
1½	teaspoons mustard powder	6	cups cooked white rice	
1	teaspoon kosher salt			

1. Melt the butter with the flour in a large stockpot over medium heat. Cook until a thick, dark red roux forms, stirring constantly with a wire whisk.

2. Add the sugar, onion, and celery and sweat for 4 minutes, until tender.

3. Add the thyme, bay leaves, the onion, garlic, and mustard powders, salt, the black and white peppers, and the cayenne and stir to coat the onion and celery.

4. Add the stock and tomatoes and bring to a boil. Reduce heat, partially cover, and simmer for 20 minutes.

5. Add the crawfish and simmer for 2 minutes to heat through.

6. Remove from heat and stir in the parsley, lemon juice, and garlic.

7. To serve, remove the bay leaves and ladle the etouffée over rice in bowls.

MAKES 12 CUPS.

LOBSTER BISQUE

VARIATION:

CRAB BISQUE
Add 1 pound of lump
crabmeat instead of
lobster. Proceed with
the recipe as directed.

ESCOFFIER'S NOTE:

The word *bisque* refers
to a highly seasoned
shellfish puree
flavored with brandy
and cream. Intensely
flavored bisques start
with a shellfish stock.
Use the shellfish but-
ter (the fat layer
on the surface of
the chilled stock) to
caramelize the vegeta-
bles. If desired, cook
a live lobster in
rapidly boiling water
for 8 minutes and use
the liquid as the base
for the stock.

4	tablespoons shellfish butter or unsalted butter
4	tablespoons all-purpose flour
3	medium white onions, chopped
2	leeks, rinsed well and chopped
2	celery stalks, chopped
1	fresh fennel bulb, chopped
2	teaspoons fennel seeds
2	bay leaves
2	teaspoons kosher salt
¼	teaspoon cayenne, or to taste
1	(28-ounce) can whole tomatoes, diced, with juice
1	bunch tarragon, stems tied together and leaves chopped
1	bunch fresh thyme, stems tied together and leaves chopped
½	cup dry vermouth
¼	cup brandy
6	cups Basic Shellfish Stock (page 225)
1½	cups heavy cream
1	pound cooked lobster meat
4	Italian plum tomatoes, seeded and diced
1	teaspoon minced fresh garlic
2	cups oyster crackers (optional)

1. Melt the shellfish butter with the flour in a large stockpot over medium heat, stirring constantly with a wire whisk. Cook until the mixture forms a thick, golden roux.

2. Add the onions, leeks, celery, and fennel bulb and sweat for 4 minutes, until tender.

3. Add the fennel seeds, bay leaves, salt, and cayenne and stir to coat the vegetables.

4. Add the canned tomatoes and tarragon and thyme stems and simmer for 5 minutes.

5. Add the vermouth and simmer for 2 minutes.

6. Add the brandy and simmer for 2 minutes.

7. Add the shellfish stock, bring the mixture to a boil, reduce heat, partially cover, and simmer for 20 minutes.

8. Reduce heat to low and add the heavy cream.

9. Remove the tarragon and thyme stems and bay leaves, puree about half of the soup in a blender or food processor, and return to the pan.

10. Add the lobster meat and simmer for 2 minutes to heat through.

11. Remove the pan from the heat and stir in the chopped tomatoes, chopped tarragon, chopped thyme, and garlic.

12. To serve, ladle the bisque into bowls and top with oyster crackers, if desired.

MAKES 12 CUPS.

REALLY DELICIOUS SOUPS

THAT DIDN'T FIT INTO ANY CHAPTER

WHEN WE DIVIDED up the soups for this book, these seven strays were left over—they didn't fit in anywhere. They were all great soups without a home. So sad. We could have named this chapter "Orphans" or "Homeless," but we didn't want to give these soups a complex.

All of these soups are actually variations on classic stews. Stewing refers to cooking meat, seafood, or vegetables in their own liquid in a covered pot. The mixture is typically simmered over long periods of time to create an intense, hearty gravy. Since we "stew" all of our soups, we have altered the definition. As a general rule, all of our soups are versatile and adaptable, much like the reversible jacket. Changing any of the ingredients shouldn't effect the outcome. If you double the amount of mussels in our Saffron Mussel Soup (page 213), you'll get more mussels per spoonful, and the flavor, although intensified, will be virtually the same. If you substitute beef for venison in our Spring Venison Goulash (page 206), you'll get the same delicious meal, you just might want to name it after another animal. And, you'll get a wider range of flavors if you use a different selection of seafood in the Bouillabaisse (page 211).

CARIBBEAN STEWED CHICKEN WITH VEGETABLES

COOK'S NOTE:

If you make this soup in advance, you may need to reconstitute it with a little water or chicken stock.
Because of the abundance of starchy vegetables, liquid is absorbed quickly when the soup is chilled.

COOK'S NOTE:

Calabaza is a round Jamaican pumpkin, usually about 5 pounds, and available in gourmet markets. Treat it as you would a regular pumpkin or any winter squash. Yuca is a shiny, dark brown root vegetable with a tough outer skin. The flesh is similar to a white potato. See Ingredient Index (page 240) for more information.

4	tablespoons peanut oil
1	whole chicken (about 4 pounds), cut up (see page 14)
10	cups mineral or filtered water
1	large Spanish onion, chopped
2	garlic cloves, minced
2	teaspoons dried thyme leaves
2	bay leaves
2	teaspoons kosher salt
½	teaspoon ground black pepper
1	(28-ounce) can whole tomatoes, drained and diced

2	white yams or potatoes, peeled, halved lengthwise, and cut into 1-inch cubes
3	cups cubed calabaza or fresh pumpkin
1	yuca, peeled, cored, and cut into 1-inch cubes
2	green plantains, sliced
¼	cup uncooked white rice
1	teaspoon habañero chile pepper sauce
½	cup chopped fresh cilantro

1. Heat 2 tablespoons of the oil in a large stockpot over medium heat. Add the chicken pieces and brown on all sides. Add water, bring to a boil, reduce heat, and simmer for 10 minutes, until chicken is cooked through. Remove the chicken with a slotted spoon, reserving the poaching liquid, and when cool enough to handle remove the meat from the bones and set aside. Strain the poaching liquid to remove solids, reserving 6 cups, and set aside.*

2. Heat the remaining 2 tablespoons of oil in the stockpot over medium heat. Add the onion and garlic and sweat for 4 minutes, until tender.

3. Add the thyme, bay leaves, salt, and pepper and stir to coat the vegetables.

4. Add the tomatoes and simmer for 2 minutes.

*To de-fat the stock, refrigerate for 1 hour, until a fat layer forms on the surface. Skim the layer of fat off the top and discard.

5. Add the chicken, reserved poaching liquid, yams, calabaza, yuca, plantains, and rice. Bring the mixture to a boil, reduce heat, partially cover, and simmer for 20 minutes, until vegetables are tender.

6. Stir in the habañero sauce and heat through.

7. To serve, remove the bay leaves, ladle the soup into bowls, and top with chopped cilantro.

MAKES 12 CUPS.

PEKING DUCK

CANTONESE
CHEF'S NOTE:

When making this
soup, think "wok"—
julienne the vegeta-
bles and quickly cook
the ingredients in a
hot pan. Stir every-
thing into simmering
broth at the end to
keep the flavors and
colors alive.

The second or third time we offered Peking Duck in our stores, a group of Chinese tourists came in and said, "We heard we should come to Daily Soup for Peking Duck." It was almost like we were Shun Lee, the famous New York City Chinese restaurant (you always hear, "When in New York, go to Shun Lee for the duck.") It was weird and wonderful at the same time. A nice affirmation of what we were trying to do.

2	tablespoons Chinese Five Spice powder	1	tablespoon minced fresh ginger
1	tablespoon Szechwan peppercorns, crushed	1	(6-inch) piece lemongrass, cut into fine julienne strips
4	teaspoons kosher salt	2	garlic cloves, thinly sliced
3	tablespoons soy sauce	½	teaspoon ground black pepper
1	whole duck (about 4–5 pounds), cut up and breasts de-boned	½	pound shiitake or porcini mushrooms, stems removed and caps thinly sliced
4	tablespoons peanut oil	1	bunch bok choy, rinsed well, greens cut crosswise, and stalks cut into fine julienne strips
10	cups mineral or filtered water		
1	large Spanish onion, chopped	1	teaspoon Sriracha hot pepper sauce*
2	carrots, peeled and cut into fine julienne strips	½	cup scallions, sliced on a bias, very thin

1. Puree 1 tablespoon of the Chinese Five Spice powder, Szechwan peppercorns, 2 teaspoons salt, and 1 tablespoon soy sauce in a blender or food processor. Transfer the mixture to a shallow dish and add the duck breasts. Press the mixture into the skin, cover with plastic, and refrigerate for 30 minutes.

*Found in Mexican specialty stores and gourmet markets.

2. Meanwhile, heat 2 tablespoons of the oil in a large stockpot over medium heat. Add the remaining duck pieces and brown on all sides. Add the water and bring to a boil. Reduce heat, partially cover, and simmer for 15 minutes, until the duck is cooked through. Strain the liquid, reserving 8 cups of the broth, and when cool enough to handle, pull the duck meat from the bones and set aside.

3. Heat the remaining 2 tablespoons of oil in the pot and add the duck breasts. Sauté until browned on both sides and medium rare in the middle (it will be slightly pink in the very center and light brown and cooked through everywhere else), about 3 minutes per side. Remove from the pan and when cool enough to handle remove the skin. Chop the skin into small pieces and return to the pan to brown and crisp. Remove the skin with a slotted spoon and set aside to use as garnish. Slice the breast crosswise into thin strips and set aside.

4. Add the onion, carrots, ginger, lemongrass, and garlic to the pot and sauté for 2 minutes.

5. Add the remaining tablespoon of Chinese Five Spice powder, remaining 2 teaspoons of salt, and the pepper and stir to coat.

6. Return the reserved broth to the pan and add the mushrooms and soy sauce. Bring to a boil, reduce heat, partially cover, and simmer for 10 minutes.

7. Remove from the heat and stir in the reserved duck breast, bok choy, and hot pepper sauce. Let stand for 2 minutes.

8. To serve, ladle the soup into bowls and top with the chopped scallions and crisp duck skin pieces.

MAKES 12 CUPS.

SPRING VENISON GOULASH

COOK'S NOTE:
We realize that there are several varieties of venison available at the market. The easiest to work with is *stewing* venison, because it's usually cut up and boneless. If you buy venison on the bone, take the potatoes out of step 6 and simmer the ingredients for 1 hour. Skim the fat from the surface, remove the meat from the bone, and return it to the pot (reserve the bones for stock or discard). Add the potatoes and simmer 20 minutes. Pick up at step 7.

4 tablespoons unsalted butter	2 tablespoons all-purpose flour
2½ pounds mushrooms (any combination of wild mushrooms), stems removed and reserved, caps sliced	2 bay leaves
	2½ teaspoons kosher salt
	1 teaspoon paprika
10 cups mineral or filtered water	½ teaspoon ground black pepper
½ cup white wine or vermouth	4 red bliss potatoes, cut into 1-inch cubes
1 pound stewing venison, cut into 1-inch cubes	1 cup fresh shelled green peas
1 large Spanish onion, chopped	½ cup heavy cream
2 celery stalks, chopped	½ cup sour cream
3 garlic cloves, minced and divided	1 tablespoon balsamic vinegar

1. Melt 2 tablespoons of the butter in a large stockpot over medium heat. Add the mushroom stems and a few mushroom caps and sweat for 5 minutes, until tender and releasing juice.
2. Add the water and wine and bring the mixture to a boil. Reduce heat, partially cover, and simmer for 20 minutes. Strain the stock through a fine sieve to remove solids, reserving 6 cups of liquid, and set aside.
3. Melt the remaining 2 tablespoons of butter in a large pot over medium heat. Add the venison, onion, celery, and 2 of the garlic cloves and sweat for 4 minutes, until tender.
4. Add the flour, bay leaves, salt, paprika, and pepper and stir to coat.
5. Add the sliced mushroom caps and cook for 2 minutes.
6. Add the reserved mushroom stock and potatoes and bring the mixture to a boil. Reduce heat, partially cover, and simmer for 20 minutes.
7. Stir in the peas and simmer for 2 minutes.
8. Reduce heat and stir in the heavy cream and sour cream.
9. Remove from heat and stir in the balsamic vinegar and remaining garlic.
10. Remove the bay leaves before serving.

MAKES 12 CUPS.

THAI HOT AND SOUR CHICKEN

3 dried Chinese woodear mushrooms, or any dried, dark wild mushroom

2 cups warm mineral or filtered water

4 tablespoons peanut oil

1 whole chicken (about 4 pounds), cut up (see page 14)

10 cups mineral or filtered water

2 garlic cloves, minced

1 tablespoon minced fresh ginger

1 (4-inch) piece lemongrass, sliced

2 Thai chilies

2 tablespoons sugar

2 teaspoons kosher salt

1 teaspoon Thai curry paste

3 shallots, thinly sliced

2 red bell peppers, seeded and chopped

1 zucchini, halved lengthwise and cut into 1-inch cubes

2 tablespoons finely minced Kaffir lime leaves

1 tablespoon fresh lemon juice

1 tablespoon fresh lime juice

½ cup chopped scallions

1. Combine the dried mushrooms and warm water and let stand for 20 minutes.

2. Heat 2 tablespoons of the oil in a large stockpot over medium heat. Add the chicken pieces and brown on all sides. Add the water, bring to a boil, reduce heat, and simmer for 10 minutes, until the chicken is cooked through. Remove the chicken with a slotted spoon, reserve the poaching liquid, and when cool enough to handle remove the meat from the bones and set aside. Strain the poaching liquid to remove solids, reserving 8 cups, and set aside.*

3. Puree the garlic, ginger, lemongrass, chilies, sugar, salt, and curry paste in a blender or food processor.

4. Heat the remaining 2 tablespoons of oil in the pot and add the garlic puree, shallots, and red peppers. Sweat for 4 minutes, until tender and golden brown.

5. Return the chicken to the pan and add the reserved stock.

*To de-fat the stock, refrigerate for 1 hour, until a fat layer forms on the surface. Skim the layer of fat off the top and discard.

COOK'S NOTE:

In Thai cuisine, limes are used to balance flavors—the sour, citrus taste is often matched up with sugar in a variety of dishes. The Kaffir lime is smaller than Western limes and the firm, shiny, bright green leaves are used in Thai cooking. We like to use the leaves, too— we just pound them with a meat mallet until they're soft and then we finely mince them. If you cannot find Kaffir lime leaves, substitute lime zest or lemongrass.

6. Drain the mushrooms, slice into thin strips, and add to the pot. Bring the mixture to a boil, reduce heat, partially cover, and simmer for 20 minutes.
7. Stir in the zucchini and lime leaves and simmer for 2 minutes.
8. Remove from heat and stir in the lemon and lime juices.
9. To serve, ladle the soup into bowls and top with chopped scallions.

MAKES 12 CUPS.

LAMB, ARTICHOKE, AND ROSEMARY STEW

5 tablespoons olive oil	2 tablespoons tomato paste
5 lamb shanks (about 1 pound each), cut into 3 pieces each	½ cup uncooked Italian farro or spelt
1 large Spanish onion, chopped	6 baby artichokes (golf-ball size), ends and tops trimmed, tough outer leaves removed (if baby artichokes are not available, substitute water-packed artichoke hearts)
2 celery stalks, chopped	
2 leeks, rinsed well and chopped	
2 garlic cloves, sliced	
1 tablespoon dried rosemary	8 cups mineral or filtered water
3 bay leaves	1 teaspoon dried thyme leaves
2 teaspoons kosher salt	1 tablespoon fresh lemon juice
4 cups Blonde Chicken Stock (page 226)	1 tablespoon balsamic vinegar
1 (28-ounce) can whole tomatoes, drained and diced	½ cup chopped scallions

1. Preheat the oven to 325 degrees.

2. Heat 4 tablespoons of the oil in a large Dutch oven over medium heat. Add the lamb shanks in batches and brown on all sides. Remove the lamb from the pot with a slotted spoon, reserving the oil in the Dutch oven, and set aside.

3. Add the onions, celery, leeks, and garlic to the pot and sweat for 4 minutes, until tender.

4. Add the rosemary, 2 of the bay leaves, and the salt and stir to coat the vegetables.

5. Return the lamb to the pot and add the chicken stock, tomatoes, and tomato paste. Bring to a boil.

6. Stir in the farro, remove from heat, cover, and place the pot in the oven. Braise for 2 hours, until the lamb is tender.

7. Meanwhile, combine the artichokes, water, remaining bay leaf, thyme, lemon juice, and 1 tablespoon olive oil in a medium saucepan over medium heat. Bring to a boil, reduce heat, partially cover, and simmer for 15 minutes, until the artichokes are tender. Remove the artichokes with a slotted spoon, reserve the stock, and when cool enough to handle, quarter the artichokes and set aside. Strain the stock to remove solids, reserving 2 cups, and set aside.

8. Remove the pot from the oven and remove the lamb shank pieces with a slotted spoon. Pull the lamb meat from the bone and return it to the pan, reserving the bones for another use.

9. Place the pot over medium heat and stir in the artichokes and reserved artichoke stock. Simmer for 2 minutes.

10. Stir in the balsamic vinegar.

11. To serve, remove the bay leaves, ladle the soup into bowls, and top with the chopped scallions.

MAKES 12 CUPS.

BOUILLABAISSE

We have several soups that are hard to pronounce. Bahian, Galician, Mulligatawny, and Bouillabaisse are just a few of the constantly mispronounced soups. Mooli-ja-tony, Booli-bahz or Ga-lick-itan are some of the funnier ones (versus the correct way: Mull-i-ga-tawny, BOY-ya-baze and GAL-ee-seeyan). Honestly, we had trouble pronouncing them at first, too. Once customers master the pronunciation, they exude confidence and even say the soup in an Indian or Spanish accent. This usually gets them free soup.

JACQUES COUSTEAU'S NOTE:

Bouillabaisse is a Provençal seafood stew flavored with garlic, fennel, saffron, and orange zest. If desired, substitute cod, mussels, lobster, and oysters for the seafood in the recipe.

2 tablespoons olive oil	4 red bliss potatoes, cut into 1-inch cubes
1 large Spanish onion, chopped	6 cups Basic Vegetable Stock (page 223)
2 celery stalks, chopped	½ pound fresh snapper, cut into 2-inch pieces
2 leeks, rinsed well and chopped	½ pound monkfish, cut into 2-inch pieces
2 garlic cloves, minced	1 pound Bay scallops
15 saffron threads	1 pound medium shrimp, peeled and deveined
2 teaspoons whole fennel seeds	½ cup dry vermouth
2 teaspoons dried thyme leaves	1 tablespoon Pernod
2 teaspoons kosher salt	½ cup chopped fresh Italian parsley
1 teaspoon grated orange zest	
½ teaspoon ground black pepper	
1 (28-ounce) can whole tomatoes, drained and diced	

1. Heat the olive oil in a large stockpot over medium heat. Add the onion, celery, leeks, and garlic and sweat for 4 minutes, until tender.

2. Add the saffron, fennel, thyme, salt, orange zest, and pepper and stir to coat the vegetables.

3. Add the tomatoes and simmer for 2 minutes.

211

4. Add the potatoes and stock and bring the mixture to a boil. Reduce heat, partially cover, and simmer for 20 minutes, until the potatoes are tender.
5. Stir in the snapper, monkfish, scallops, and shrimp and simmer for 3 minutes.
6. Remove from heat and stir in the vermouth and Pernod.
7. To serve, ladle the soup into bowls and top with the chopped parsley.

MAKES 12 CUPS.

SAFFRON MUSSEL

24 mussels, shells tightly closed, beards
    removed and scrubbed
2 cups mineral or filtered water
½ cup dry vermouth
2 shallots, chopped
2 tablespoons unsalted butter
1 large Spanish onion, chopped
2 celery stalks, chopped
2 leeks, rinsed well and chopped
2 garlic cloves, minced
2 teaspoons dried thyme leaves

2 teaspoons whole fennel seeds
2 bay leaves
2 teaspoons kosher salt
¼ teaspoon cayenne
2 cups Basic Vegetable Stock (page
    223)
1 (28-ounce) can whole tomatoes, diced
4 red bliss potatoes, cut into 1-inch
    cubes
1 cup heavy cream
15 saffron threads

SPANISH FLORIST'S NOTE:
Saffron threads are the whole dried stigmas of the autumn crocus, a beautiful, violet-colored flower. Known as the world's most expensive spice, it takes about 75,000 flowers to produce just one pound of saffron. Thankfully, a little goes a long way. Steeping the threads in hot liquid (cream) releases and intensifies the characteristic aroma and flavor.

1. Combine the mussels, water, vermouth, and shallots in a large stockpot over medium heat. Bring to a boil, cover, and steam until the shells open, about 5 minutes. Remove the mussels with a slotted spoon, reserve the broth, and discard any shells that have not opened. When cool enough to handle, remove the mussels from the shells, remove and discard the dark sac, and set the mussels aside (discard shells). Strain the broth to remove solids and set aside.

2. Melt the butter in a large stockpot over medium heat. Add the onion, celery, leeks, and garlic and sweat for 4 minutes, until tender.

3. Add the thyme, fennel seeds, bay leaves, salt, and cayenne and stir to coat the vegetables.

4. Add the reserved broth, mussels, stock, tomatoes, and potatoes. Bring to a boil, reduce heat, partially cover, and simmer for 20 minutes, until the potatoes are tender.

5. Meanwhile, combine the heavy cream and saffron in a small saucepan over medium heat. Simmer until reduced by half.

6. Puree the cream and saffron in a blender until smooth.

7. Stir the saffron cream into the pot and simmer for 1 minute to heat through.

8. To serve, remove the bay leaves, ladle the soup into bowls, and top with the chopped parsley.

MAKES 12 CUPS.

THINGS TO DO WITH LEFTOVER SOUP

TOMATO-BASIL "CREAMSICLE": Puree the soup with a sprinkle of sugar. Transfer the mixture to ice trays, add toothpicks, and freeze.

CRAB CORN CHOWDER CAKES: Mix the soup with bread crumbs, eggs, and sliced scallions. Form into cakes, dredge in cornmeal, and fry in hot oil.

CHICKEN POT PIE CASSEROLE: Mix the soup with cooked egg noodles and bake at 350 degrees for 1 hour.

PEA PARMESAN PUDDING: Add more parmesan and 4 eggs. Transfer the mixture to a baking dish and bake at 350 degrees for 30 minutes.

ROASTED EGGPLANT PARMESAN HERO: Spoon the soup between two sides of a torpedo roll.

AVOCADO AND GRILLED SHRIMP SALSA: Strain the liquid from the soup, add diced tomatoes, scallions, and hot habañero sauce. Serve with corn chips.

GREEN GUMBO WITH OYSTER PO' BOY: This is a very Po' Boy—no frying necessary. Make a sandwich.

LOBSTER BISQUE EGGS BENEDICT: Using a slotted spoon, remove the lobster from the soup. Make hollandaise sauce and stir into the bisque. Assemble the lobster meat on English muffin halves and top with the hollandaise-bisque mixture.

JAMAICAN PUMPKIN PIE: Add three eggs and ½ cup of heavy cream to the soup. Pour the mixture into an unbaked pie shell and bake at 325 degrees for 1 hour, until set.

CHILI CON CARNE NACHOS: This one needs no explanation. Don't forget the pickled jalapeños.

BURMESE SHRIMP CURRY FRIED RICE: Stir-fry cooked rice in peanut oil. Stir into the soup and heat through.

TURKEY WHITE BEAN CHILI MEAT LOAF: Add 8 slices of milk-soaked bread and 2 eggs. Transfer the mixture to a 9-inch bread pan and bake at 350 degrees for 1 hour.

MOO SHOO PEKING DUCK: Strain the liquid from the soup and serve the duck and vegetables with Chinese pancakes and plum or hoisin sauce.

CAULIFLOWER BREAD SALAD: Strain the liquid from the soup, reserving the cauliflower. Make a vinaigrette dressing with garlic, balsamic vinegar, and extra virgin olive oil. Toss the vinaigrette with the reserved cauliflower and toasted or fresh cubed bread.

REFRIED CUBAN BLACK BEANS: Sauté the soup in vegetable oil or bacon drippings.

ALPINE CHEESE FONDUE: Add more cheese and melt in a fondue pot. Serve with cubed bread and sliced apples.

FRENCH ONION DIP: Simmer the soup until the liquid completely evaporates. Simmer until the mixture becomes a thick syrup. Add sour cream when cooled and serve with fresh vegetables and chips.

FROZEN CUCUMBER YOGURT: Puree the soup with honey. Transfer the mixture to a shallow baking dish and freeze until firm. When frozen, puree again until smooth.

STUFFED BAKED POTATO WITH CHEDDAR CHEESE WITH POTATOES AND BACON: Bake potatoes until tender. Halve, scoop out the center, and mix with the soup. Return the soup mixture to the baked potatoes and bake at 350 degrees for 20 minutes.

MALAYSIAN CABBAGE AND PEANUT SLAW: Strain the liquid from the soup and reduce it until it becomes a thick syrup. Toss the soup solids with rice vinegar and stir in the thickened syrup.

THAI CHILLED MELON JELLO: Puree the soup, add gelatin, and chill until firm.

LAMB, ARTICHOKE, AND ROSEMARY FOCACCIA: Strain the liquid from the soup. Assemble solids on ready-made pizza crust. Bake at 400 degrees for 20 minutes.

VENISON RED BEAN CHILI LASAGNA: Add ricotta cheese to the soup. Spoon the mixture between lasagna noodles and top with grated mozzarella. Cover with foil and bake at 350 degrees for 1 hour.

MUSHROOM POT PIE STUFFING: Add day-old cubed bread. Spoon into chicken or turkey and roast as directed.

BABY NAMES FOR THE NEW MILLENNIUM

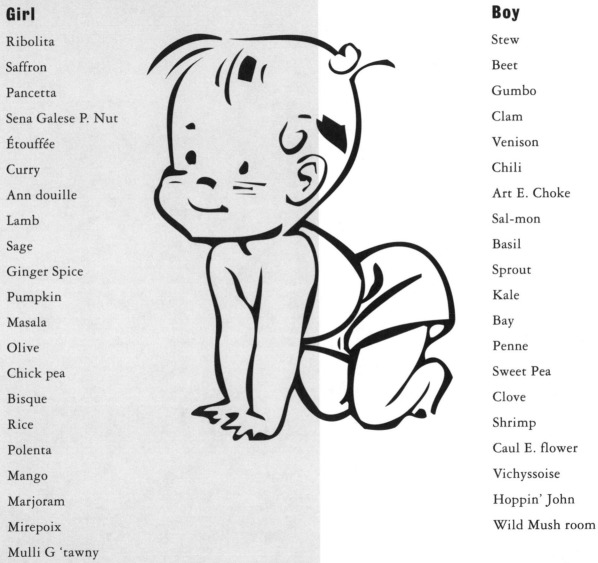

Girl

Ribolita
Saffron
Pancetta
Sena Galese P. Nut
Étouffée
Curry
Ann douille
Lamb
Sage
Ginger Spice
Pumpkin
Masala
Olive
Chick pea
Bisque
Rice
Polenta
Mango
Marjoram
Mirepoix
Mulli G 'tawny

Boy

Stew
Beet
Gumbo
Clam
Venison
Chili
Art E. Choke
Sal-mon
Basil
Sprout
Kale
Bay
Penne
Sweet Pea
Clove
Shrimp
Caul E. flower
Vichyssoise
Hoppin' John
Wild Mush room

STOCKS

IN THE CHINESE language they use the same word for soup as they do for stock. We use two different words, but a good stock makes a good soup. Typically, stock is the flavored essence of meat, fish and shellfish, and vegetables. It's the foundation for soup, so it's extremely important that the flavors be balanced. For the best stock, you need to extract every ounce of flavor from the bones, vegetables, and herbs. The longer and slower meat stocks are cooked, the better the flavor. Vegetable, fish, and shellfish stocks have shorter cooking times because they become bitter and fishy when cooked too long. Additionally, the more ingredients you add, the richer the broth. We use filtered water in our stocks, but since you're boiling everything, tap water is fine.

Every soup needs a stock, it's like their "blankie." If you don't feel like making stock, choose a soup that uses dried beans or lentils because they make their own flavorful broth as they soften. And, there's always the canned broth option. But, trust us, make your own stock once, and you'll quickly discover the difference.

A WORD ABOUT STOCKS

- ☞ START WITH COLD WATER
- ☞ DON'T STIR
- ☞ DON'T RUSH
- ☞ SIMMER, DON'T BOIL
- ☞ DON'T COVER
- ☞ DON'T SWIM WITHOUT A LIFEGUARD PRESENT

To de-fat stock, refrigerate it until a fat layer forms on the top (at least 1 hour). Then, just spoon off the layer of fat and discard it (or use it to sauté vegetables in another recipe). Blot any remaining surface fat with a paper towel.

Many of the soups in this book have stocks incorporated right into their recipes, including stocks made with Parmesan rinds, corn, shallots, onions, beans, clams, asparagus, mushrooms, artichokes, and various Asian ingredients. This chapter includes several basic stocks, a few flavor-infused basic stocks, and some unusual stock concoctions.

Stocks will keep in the refrigerator for up to two weeks and in the freezer for up to two months. There's no need to thaw stock before using it, just reheat it in a large stockpot and proceed with the recipe as directed. Great tip: Freeze stock in ice cube trays and pop them out as needed. You can store these in sealed freezer bags. Once stock has been frozen, thawed, and reheated, use it up as refreezing diminishes flavor.

BASIC VEGETABLE STOCK

1   large Spanish onion, chopped
3   carrots, peeled and chopped
4   celery stalks with leaves, chopped
2   whole tomatoes, chopped
1   leek, chopped
½   head garlic

⅓   cup white wine
12   cups mineral or filtered water
1½   teaspoons kosher salt
¼   teaspoon whole peppercorns
1   Bouquet Garni (page 233)

1. Combine all the ingredients in a large stockpot.
2. Bring to a boil over medium-high heat.
3. Reduce heat, partially cover, and simmer for 1 hour.
4. Strain the stock and discard solids.

MAKES 12 CUPS.

VARIATION:
ASIAN-INFUSED
VEGETABLE STOCK
Add a 6-inch piece of
ginger root, 1 head
of garlic, 1 stalk of
lemongrass, 6 Chi-
nese dried mushrooms
(or any dried, dark
wild mushroom), 6
scallions, 1 serrano
chile, 1 tablespoon of
whole black pepper-
corns, and 1 table-
spoon of lightly
crushed Szechwan
peppercorns.

VARIATION:
PARMESAN STOCK
Add a 3-inch piece of
Parmesan cheese rind.

INDIAN VEGETABLE STOCK

3   tablespoons ghee* or vegetable oil

2   small onions, unpeeled, quartered

1   carrot, chopped

2   garlic cloves, unpeeled

1   (1-inch) piece fresh ginger

2   teaspoons coriander seeds

1   teaspoon cumin seeds

1   cinnamon stick

3   black, or 6 green, cardamom pods

8   whole cloves

1   teaspoon whole black peppercorns

1   teaspoon kosher salt

12   cups mineral or filtered water

1. Heat the ghee in a large stockpot over medium heat.

2. Add all of the ingredients except the water and sauté for 10 minutes, until the spices are fragrant and the onions are golden brown.

3. Add the water and bring to a boil.

4. Reduce heat, partially cover, and simmer for 2 hours.

5. Strain the mixture through a fine sieve to remove solids.

6. Refrigerate until ready to use.

MAKES 12 CUPS.

*Ghee is clarified butter that's allowed to simmer for several hours over lower heat, allowing the sugars in the butter to caramelize and produce a nutty flavor. The advantage to cooking with ghee is that it doesn't burn like butter. You can prepare your own by simmering butter over low heat until the butterfat, water, and milk separate, forming 2 distinct layers (about 10 to 15 minutes). Allow to simmer for another 30 minutes to 1 hour. Strain the liquid from the solids and store the clear yellow liquid in the refrigerator until solid. This stock can be frozen up to 2 months. Use as directed.

BASIC SHELLFISH STOCK

8   tablespoons unsalted butter, softened
2   pounds crustacean shells (shrimp, crab, lobster, crawfish), preferably with heads on
2   tablespoons olive oil
1   large Spanish onion, chopped
1   carrot, chopped
1   celery stalk with leaves, chopped
1   leek, chopped
½   head garlic
2   ripe tomatoes, halved
1   teaspoon whole black peppercorns
4   sprigs fresh Italian parsley
4   sprigs fresh tarragon
2   sprigs fresh thyme
1   sprig fresh rosemary
1   cup white wine
1   cup brandy
12 cups mineral or filtered water

1. To make a shellfish butter, divide the butter and crustacean shells into 4 equal parts. Process one part of each (butter and shells) in a blender or food processor until the shells are finely crushed and the butter is incorporated. Repeat with the remaining 3 batches.
2. Heat the olive oil in a large stockpot over medium heat.
3. Add the shellfish butter and sauté for 4 minutes, until the mixture appears dry.
4. Add the onion, carrot, celery, leek, garlic, tomatoes, peppercorns, and fresh herbs. Simmer until the liquid is absorbed.
5. Add the white wine and simmer until the liquid is absorbed.
6. Add the brandy and simmer until the liquid is absorbed.
7. Add the water, bring to a boil, reduce heat, partially cover, and simmer for 1 hour.
8. Strain the stock through a fine sieve, pressing the shells and vegetables with the back of a spoon to extract all the juice.
9. Chill.
10. Remove the butter layer from the surface and reserve for another use, such as using in place of butter or oil in sautéing.

MAKES 12 CUPS.

BLONDE CHICKEN STOCK

Blonde stocks definitely have more fun.

2 pounds chicken backs and necks
12 cups mineral or filtered water
1 large Spanish onion, chopped
2 celery stalks with leaves, chopped

2 carrots, chopped
½ cup white wine
1 teaspoon kosher salt
½ teaspoon whole black peppercorns

1. Combine all the ingredients in a large stockpot.
2. Bring to a boil over medium-high heat, reduce heat, partially cover, and simmer for 1 hour.
3. Strain the stock and discard solids.
4. Refrigerate until ready to use.

MAKES 12 CUPS.

FORTIFIED CHICKEN STOCK

2 chicken carcasses, chopped	1 stalk celery, chopped
½ calf's foot, chopped	2 onions, chopped
12 cups mineral or filtered water	1 carrot, chopped
1 teaspoon whole black peppercorns, lightly crushed	2 tomatoes, chopped
	½ cup white wine
1 leek, chopped	1 Bouquet Garni (page 233)

1. In a large stockpot, combine the carcasses and enough water to cover.
2. Bring to a boil and cook for 5 minutes.
3. Drain.
4. Return the chicken bones to the stockpot and add the calf's foot and 12 cups water.
5. Bring to a boil, skimming frequently.
6. When the liquid reaches a full boil, add the peppercorns, vegetables, wine, and Bouquet Garni.
7. Reduce the heat, partially cover, and simmer for 4 hours, skimming frequently to remove surface foam.
8. Strain through a fine sieve to remove solids and refrigerate for 1 hour.
9. Remove the fat layer from the surface and refrigerate until ready to use.

MAKES 12 CUPS.

LAMB STOCK

2	pounds lamb bones	2	tomatoes, chopped
3	tablespoons olive oil	½	calf's foot, chopped
2	onions, chopped	½	cup dry red wine
1	leek, chopped	12	cups mineral or filtered water
1	stalk celery, chopped	1	teaspoon whole peppercorns, lightly crushed
1	carrot, chopped	1	Bouquet Garni (page 233)
½	head garlic, unpeeled		

1. Preheat the oven to 400 degrees.
2. Combine the lamb bones and oil in a large roasting pan and stir to coat the bones.
3. Roast for 1 hour, stirring regularly.
4. Add the onions, leek, celery, carrot, garlic, and tomatoes and roast 30 minutes, stirring regularly.
5. Transfer the bones and vegetables to a large stockpot and add the calf's foot and red wine. Simmer over medium heat for 5 minutes, stirring to incorporate brown bits into the wine.
6. Add the water and bring mixture to a boil.
7. Add the peppercorns and Bouquet Garni, reduce heat, partially cover, and simmer for 4 hours, skimming the surface frequently to remove foam.
8. Strain the mixture to remove solids.
9. Refrigerate until ready to use.

MAKES 12 CUPS.

BEEF STOCK

1	large onion, unpeeled and halved	1	teaspoon whole cloves
2	pounds beef bones	1	teaspoon kosher salt
1	bay leaf	12	cups mineral or filtered water
1	teaspoon whole black peppercorns		

1. Combine all ingredients in a large stockpot over medium heat.
2. Bring to a boil, reduce heat, partially cover, and simmer for 4 hours, skimming the top frequently.
3. Strain the liquid to remove solids.
4. Refrigerate for 1 hour.
5. Remove the fat layer from the surface and refrigerate until ready to use.

MAKES 12 CUPS.

BASIC FISH STOCK

2 pounds fresh fish bones, from white, nonoily fish

12 cups mineral or filtered water

½ cup white wine

10 whole black peppercorns

1 large onion, unpeeled and chopped

3 (1-inch) slices fresh ginger

2 celery stalks, chopped

1 carrot, chopped

1. Combine all the ingredients in a large stockpot over medium heat.

2. Bring to a boil, reduce heat, partially cover, and simmer for 2 hours.

3. Strain the liquid to remove solids.

4. Refrigerate until ready to use.

MAKES 12 CUPS.

ASIAN FISH STOCK

2 tablespoons peanut oil
2 small yellow onions, chopped
2 celery stalks, chopped
2 (1-inch) pieces fresh ginger
1 small green serrano chile, halved
2 pounds fresh fish bones from white, nonoily fish

12 cups mineral or filtered water
2 cups white wine
1 cup Chinese rice wine or dry sherry
1 teaspoon kosher salt

1. Heat the oil in a large stockpot over medium heat. Add the onions, celery, ginger, and serrano and sauté for 4 minutes, until golden.
2. Add the fish bones and sweat for 10 minutes.
3. Add the remaining ingredients and bring the mixture to a boil. Reduce heat, partially cover, and simmer for 1 hour.
4. Strain the liquid to remove solids and refrigerate until ready to use.

MAKES 12 CUPS.

CONCOCTIONS, GARNISHES, AND OTHER POTIONS

MIREPOIX VARIATIONS

A *mirepoix* is a combination of chopped aromatic vegetables. The vegetables are often "sweated" in butter or oil and then used as the base for stocks, soups, and stews.

STANDARD MIREPOIX

1   large Spanish onion, chopped
2   celery stalks, chopped

2   carrots, peeled and chopped

WHITE MIREPOIX

1   large Spanish onion, chopped
4   garlic cloves, minced

2   leeks, rinsed well and chopped
2   celery stalks, chopped

INDIAN MIREPOIX

1   large Spanish onion, chopped
2   garlic cloves, *pureed with*

1   tablespoon minced fresh ginger

THAI MIREPOIX

3 shallots, thinly sliced
2 garlic cloves, *pureed with*

1 tablespoon minced fresh ginger
1 teaspoon Thai curry paste

SOUTHWESTERN MIREPOIX

3 small white onions, chopped
2 celery stalks, chopped

1 green bell pepper, seeded and chopped

CHOWDER MIREPOIX

1 large Spanish onion, chopped
2 celery stalks, chopped

HERB AND SPICE MIXTURES
BOUQUET GARNI

3 fresh Italian parsley sprigs
1 fresh thyme sprig

1 bay leaf

1. Combine all the ingredients on a piece of cheesecloth.
2. Fold up and secure tightly with a piece of string.
3. Use as directed.

STANDARD CHILI POWDER

1   dried ancho chile pepper, crushed
2   tablespoons chili powder
1   tablespoon dried Mexican oregano
    (see Ingredient Index, page 240), or
    regular dried oregano

2   teaspoons ground cumin seeds
1½ teaspoons ground coriander seeds
2   bay leaves
2   teaspoons kosher salt

1. Grind all the ingredients together in a coffee grinder or with a mortar and pestle.
2. Store in an airtight container until ready to use.

GREEK-INFUSED CHILI POWDER

2   tablespoons chili powder
1   tablespoon oregano
1½ teaspoons ground coriander seeds
¼   teaspoon ground cinnamon
¼   teaspoon ground allspice

¼   teaspoon ground cloves
¼   teaspoon cayenne
2   bay leaves
2   teaspoons kosher salt

1. Grind all the ingredients together in a spice mill, coffee grinder, blender, or
   with a mortar and pestle.
2. Store in an airtight container until ready to use.

CAJUN SEASONING FOR GUMBOS

2   teaspoons dried thyme leaves

2   bay leaves

2   teaspoons kosher salt

1½ teaspoons onion powder

1½ teaspoons garlic powder

1½ teaspoons mustard powder

1½ teaspoons ground turmeric

½   teaspoon ground black pepper

½   teaspoon ground white pepper

½   teaspoon cayenne

1. Combine all the ingredients and store in an airtight container until ready to use.

STANDARD GARAM MASALA

1   tablespoon whole cardamom

1   tablespoon whole coriander seeds

1   tablespoon cumin seeds

1   cinnamon stick

1   teaspoon whole cloves

½   teaspoon black peppercorns

¼   teaspoon grated nutmeg

2   bay leaves

1. Preheat the oven to 300 degrees.
2. Grind all the ingredients together in a spice mill, blender, coffee grinder, or with a mortar and pestle until fine.
3. Place in an oven-proof skillet and roast for 10 minutes.
4. Use as directed.

FRAGRANT GARAM MASALA

3 cinnamon sticks	1 teaspoon whole cloves
2 teaspoons cardamom seeds	1 teaspoon grated mace blades

1. Preheat the oven to 300 degrees.
2. Place the spices in an oven-proof skillet and roast for 10 minutes.
3. Grind together in a spice mill, blender, coffee grinder, or with a mortar and pestle until fine.

KASHMIRI GARAM MASALA

2 teaspoons cardamom seeds	1 cinnamon stick
1 teaspoon black or yellow cumin seeds	½ teaspoon whole cloves
1 teaspoon whole black peppercorns	¼ teaspoon grated nutmeg

1. Preheat the oven to 300 degrees.
2. Place all the spices but the nutmeg in an oven-proof skillet and roast for 10 minutes.
3. Transfer to a spice mill, blender, coffee grinder, or mortar and pestle, add the nutmeg, and grind until fine.

PICKLED JALAPEÑOS

12 jalapeño peppers, stem ends trimmed
     and halved crosswise
2   cups distilled white vinegar

1   tablespoon kosher salt
½   teaspoon cayenne pepper

COOK'S NOTE:
Pickled jalapeños
can be stored in the
refrigerator for up to
one month.

1. Combine all the ingredients in a sealable container.
2. Refrigerate for at least 3 days before using.

BASIL PESTO

1½ cups tightly packed fresh basil leaves
½   cup grated Parmesan cheese
¼   cup lightly toasted pine nuts

2   garlic cloves
½   cup olive oil

1. Combine the basil, Parmesan, pine nuts, garlic, and salt in a blender or food processor.
2. Process until finely chopped.
3. With the motor running, gradually add the olive oil and process until a smooth paste forms.

ROUILLE SAUCE

2 medium red bell peppers
4 thick slices of a dry baguette, broken up
6 garlic cloves, minced

1 teaspoon cayenne
1 teaspoon kosher salt
¾ cup olive oil

1. Preheat the broiler.
2. Place the red peppers under the broiler, 4 inches from the heat source, and char on all sides (or roast peppers over a flame of a gas burner). When blackened on all sides, remove from the broiler and place in a paper or plastic bag for 5 minutes to steam. Remove from the bag, peel away the charred skin, halve, seed, and chop; set aside.
3. To make the sauce, soak the bread slices in water to soften, then squeeze dry.
4. Combine the bread, roasted red peppers, garlic, cayenne, and salt in a blender or food processor. Puree until smooth.
5. With the motor running, gradually add the olive oil in a steady stream until blended and smooth.

MAKES 1 CUP.

AIOLI

*A*ioli is a garlic mayonnaise that can be spread on bread, toast, and croutons before serving with soup. It's important to use fresh, juicy garlic cloves for the best outcome.

6	large garlic cloves	2	large egg yolks, room temperature
½	teaspoon kosher salt	1	cup extra virgin olive oil

1. Using a mortar and pestle or the flat side of a knife, crush together garlic and salt. Mash together to form a paste.
2. Add 1 egg yolk and stir, pressing slowly and evenly with the pestle or a wire whisk until thoroughly blended.
3. Add the second yolk and mix until well blended.
4. Gradually add the olive oil and stir constantly until the mixture thickens to the consistency of mayonnaise.

MAKES 1 CUP.

INGREDIENT INDEX

ACHIOTE PASTE: A thick, reddish brown paste made from the ground seeds of the annatto tree. Available in Mexican specialty stores and gourmet markets.

AVOCADO LEAF: The large dried leaf of the avocado (at least two times the size of a dried bay leaf), with a strong avocado/bay leaf flavor. Available in Mexican specialty stores and gourmet markets.

BLACK LENTILS: Tiny black lentils (like Beluga caviar) that hold their shape when cooked. They are used extensively in Indian cuisine. Available in gourmet markets and Indian specialty stores.

CALABAZA: A round Jamaican pumpkin. Available in gourmet markets.

CALF'S FOOT: Literally the whole foot of a calf (be prepared, it's a bit shocking). Available by special request at butcher shops and gourmet markets.

CHINESE FIVE-SPICE: A licorice-scented powder made with star anise, Szechwan peppercorns, fennel, cinnamon, and cloves. Available in supermarkets, gourmet markets, and Asian specialty stores.

CHINESE WATERCRESS: Watercress with longer, more narrow leaves than the European version. The leaves and stems have a fresh, peppery taste and bold, green color. Available in gourmet markets.

CHIPOTLE IN ADOBO: Dried and smoked jalapeños in tomato sauce (adobo). Available in gourmet markets and Mexican specialty stores.

CHORIZO: The most typical Spanish sausage, heavily scented with paprika and garlic. Sliced chorizo can be eaten cold or added to soups, stews, and main dishes. Available in supermarkets and gourmet food stores.

COCONUT MILK: Milk made from freshly grated pulp, steeped in boiling water. Buy the unsweetened varieties. Available in cans in supermarkets and gourmet food stores.

CRANBERRY OR BORLOTTI BEANS: A putty-colored bean with burgundy markings. Tastes like a flavorful kidney bean, and the skin turns pinkish brown when cooked. Available in gourmet markets and Italian specialty stores.

DRIED CHIPOTLE: Dried and smoked jalapeño peppers. Available in gourmet markets and Mexican specialty stores.

DRIED SHRIMP: A key ingredient in Thai sauces, curries, and salads. Made from drying shrimp by salting, then exposing shrimp to the sun. Be prepared, they smell a bit fishy. Available both whole and ground in Asian specialty stores and gourmet markets.

EPAZOTE: A Mexican wild herb with a marjoram/oreganolike flavor. Available in Mexican specialty stores and gourmet markets.

FRESH FAVA BEAN: Also known as horse or broad bean. Large, flat bean with inedible pod. Available in the produce section of most gourmet markets.

FILÉ POWDER: The ground bark of the sassafras tree. Used extensively in Creole gumbos as a distinct, earthy thickener. Available in gourmet markets.

GARAM MASALA: An Indian spice blend of cardamom, coriander, cumin, cinnamon, cloves, black pepper, and nutmeg. Available in gourmet markets and Indian specialty stores.

ITALIAN FARRO OR SPELT: A mild-flavored grain from Tuscany, similar to barley, wheatberries, and bulgur. Available in gourmet markets.

KAFFIR LIME LEAF: The leaves of the Thai Kaffir lime (*citrushysterix*). Strong lemon-lime flavor used in a variety of dishes. Available in Asian specialty stores and gourmet markets.

KOSHER SALT: Also known as coarse salt, kosher salt is actually rough grains of salt that impart less of a "salty" taste to soup.

LEMONGRASS: A tough, reedlike plant with a strong lemon aroma and flavor. The tough outer stalks and roots should be removed before chopping and cooking. Available in gourmet markets and Asian specialty stores.

MEXICAN OREGANO: A stronger oregano flavor than traditional oregano. Available in Mexican specialty stores and gourmet markets.

MIRIN: Rice wine with an 8 percent alcohol content and a significant amount of sugar. Available in Asian specialty stores and gourmet markets.

PURPLE POTATOES: Also known as the Purple Peruvian and purple fingerling.

They have purple skin and beautiful, purple flesh. Available in supermarkets and gourmet food stores.

QUESO BLANCO: A mild farmers cheese with a Monterey Jack/feta cheese combination of flavors. Available in Mexican specialty stores and gourmet markets.

SAFFRON: Saffron threads are the whole dried stigmas of the autumn crocus, a beautiful, violet-colored flower. Known as the world's most expensive spice, it takes about 75,000 flowers to produce just one pound of saffron. Steeping the threads in hot liquid (cream) releases and intensifies the characteristic aroma and flavor.

SAUÇISSON A L'AIL: A smoke-cured pork sausage made with garlic, white wine, and spices. Available in gourmet markets.

SHRIMP PASTE: A thick paste consisting of dried shrimp, salt, and spices. Available in Asian specialty stores and gourmet markets.

SRIRACHA CHILI SAUCE: Hot sauce made with red chilies, sugar, garlic, salt, and vinegar. Available in Asian specialty stores and gourmet markets.

SZECHWAN PEPPERCORNS: Dried, reddish-brown berries with a woodsy-spicy flavor. Not related to black peppercorns or chili peppers. Available in gourmet markets and Asian specialty stores.

TANDOORI SPICE MIX: An Indian spice combination consisting of garlic, ginger, coriander, cumin, red pepper, cinnamon, and turmeric. Available in Indian specialty stores and gourmet markets.

TASSO: A heavily spiced and smoked cured ham made primarily from the pork shoulder. First cured in salt brine, then rubbed with spices and cold-smoked until very dry. Used extensively in Creole and Cajun cooking. Available in gourmet markets.

THAI CURRY PASTE: A thick paste consisting of chilies, garlic, and seasonings. Used as the basis for classic curries and available in four varieties—red, green, *Massaman*, and *Panaeng*. Available in Asian specialty stores and gourmet markets.

THAI FISH SAUCE: Also known as *nahm pla* in Thailand. Made from fish and prawns that have been fermented in salt. A light brown sauce that's common in many Thai dishes, especially salads. Available in gourmet markets and Asian specialty stores.

THAI RED CHILI PEPPERS: Small red chilies with a pungent, spicy flavor. Be careful, they're hot. Available in Asian specialty stores and gourmet markets.

WHITE YAM: Tropical root vegetable with crisp, bland white to yellow flesh. Available in gourmet markets and Hispanic specialty stores.

YUCA ROOT: Also known as cassava, manioc, or tapioca. Shiny, barklike outer skin with pure white flesh similar to a flaky boiled potato. Available in gourmet markets.

INGREDIENT SOURCES

**International Foods
543 Ninth Avenue Corp.**

Imported and Domestic Gourmet Foods
543 Ninth Avenue
New York, NY 10018
(212) 279-1000

The Spanish Table

1427 Western Avenue
Seattle, WA 98101
(206) 682-2827
fax (206) 682-2814
E-mail: tablespan@aol.com

Thailand Friendship Corp.

(212) 349-1979

Foods of India

(212) 683-4419

ACKNOWLEDGMENTS

IT ALL STARTED in a small East Village kitchen one cool February weekend in 1995. Bob, Carla, and I were trying to put into words the passion, energy, and excitement we feel for soup. At the time, it was an extremely difficult task. When it comes to soup, it is much easier to do than describe. So we spent an intensive forty-eight hours of cooking, tasting, playing, questioning, and enjoying.

Daily Soup has come quite a long way since this infamous weekend. Leslie Kaul joined us not so long after that and has since helped develop some of our most exciting soups. She and Bob have steadfastly pursued a challenging goal: to make the finest soups that are substantial enough to eat as a meal, with the absolute best quality ingredients—prepared by hand every day the way Grandma used to.

The recipes in this book are a result of intense amounts of hard work, dedication, passion, and expertise on the subject of soup. Leslie and Bob deserve more credit than this page allows. Thank you, Bob. Thank you, Leslie.

—Peter

WE WOULD ALSO like to extend thanks to: Mary and Oakley Spiegel. Carla's husband Georgios Avramopoulos. The Spiegels: Herb, Jon, Suz, Ade, Matt, Tom, Shana, Jack, Joan, and Ida. The Rubens: Herb, Ernie, Flip, Lisa, and Erica, for all their belief. The Siegels: Marty, Denny, Hank, Lissette, Andrew, Ben, Jeff, Heidi, Emily, Ellie, Scott, Lucy, and Oliver. To Leslie's mother Sue—without whom we wouldn't have Leslie. Jon Stewart and Tracey for letting Bob distract their vacation. Mr. (Dan) Popkin of Daniel Popkin Enterprises, Creative Edge Parties, Will Schwalbe for his great dental work, Halley MacNaughton for all her patience, Mollie Doyle, Dave Conway, Alex Dzieduszycki (sche-shoo-chitski), Dana Sinkler, Harold Lewis, Rodrigo Benedon Oks, Celine Beitchman, Javier Tepale, Clifford Public Relations, Rich O'Donnell, Mabel Chan, Alan Cohen, Sid Feltenstein, Laura Paresky, and mothers all over the world. Thank you.

ABOUT THE AUTHORS

Leslie Kaul attended the celebrated French Culinary Institute in Manhattan and, upon graduation, entered the fiercely competitive world of top-flight New York restaurants. After working her way through the ranks at Union Square Café, she went on to assume the prestigious saucier position at Lespinasse, eventually leaving to become a sous-chef at Gramercy Tavern. As Kaul's reputation grew, she came to the attention of Bob Spiegel and, in the fall of 1996, was enlisted as chef for Bob's new venture, Daily Soup.

Carla Ruben has been involved in the food business for over ten years. She and Bob own one of New York's premier catering companies, Creative Edge Parties Caterers, Inc. With the experience of serving thousands of people came the concept and expertise needed to launch Daily Soup. Ruben resides in New York with her husband Georgios Avramopoulos.

Peter Siegel is an enigma.

Bob Spiegel was born in Trenton, New Jersey, and is CEO of Daily Soup. He graduated from Johnson and Wales College in 1982. He went on to become the sous-chef of New York's Glorious Food and co-founded Creative Edge Parties with Carla Ruben. In 1986, he was asked to teach American cuisine to chefs from the top hotel restaurants in India in exchange for their culinary secrets. He has also cooked extensively in the Emilia Romana and Tuscany regions of Italy, mainland China, and Hong Kong.

Robin Vitetta-Miller is a food writer and nutritionist whose other books include *Jane Fonda Cooking for Healthy Living* and *The Newlywed Cookbook.* She is a contributing editor for *Cooking Light* and has frequent food and nutrition features in *Shape, Health, Natural Health,* and *Men's Fitness.* She makes regular guest appearances on local, network, and cable television, providing nutrition information and conducting cooking demonstrations. Robin and her husband, Darrin, reside in Princeton, New Jersey.

INDEX